RACHEL BILLUPS

AN
UNLIKELY
LENT

EXTRAORDINARY PEOPLE OF
THE EASTER STORY

Abingdon Press | Nashville

An Unlikely Lent
Extraordinary People of the Easter Story

Library of Congress Control Number: 2025946599
978-1-7910-3733-8

Cover Description: Background is dark purple with a decorative floral border. At the top is a crown of thorns, and at the bottom a small rooster. Title reads *An Unlikely Lent* in large white letters. Below are white silhouettes of a donkey, an open tomb with the stone rolled away, a dove, and three crosses on a hill. Subtitle reads *Extraordinary People of the Easter Story* by Rachel Billups.

To my children—
AJ, Topher, David, Sarah

Keep wrestling with your faith and
the sacred words of Scripture.
Stay curious.

An Unlikely Lent
Extraordinary People
of the Easter Story

An Unlikely Lent
978-1-7910-3733-8
978-1-7910-3735-2 eBook

An Unlikely Lent: DVD
978-1-7910-3737-6

An Unlikely Lent: Leader Guide
978-1-7910-3734-5
978-1-7910-3736-9 eBook

CONTENTS

Introduction vii

1. Unlikely Offering: Mary of Bethany 1

2. Unlikely Opposition: The Servant Girl 21

3. Unlikely Freedom: Barabbas 43

4. Unlikely Companionship: Simon of Cyrene 63

5. Unlikely Courage: The Women at the Cross 83

6. Unlikely Allies: Joseph of Arimathea and Nicodemus . . . 103

Epilogue 123

Notes. 130

View a complimentary session
of Rachel Billup's
An Unlikely Lent

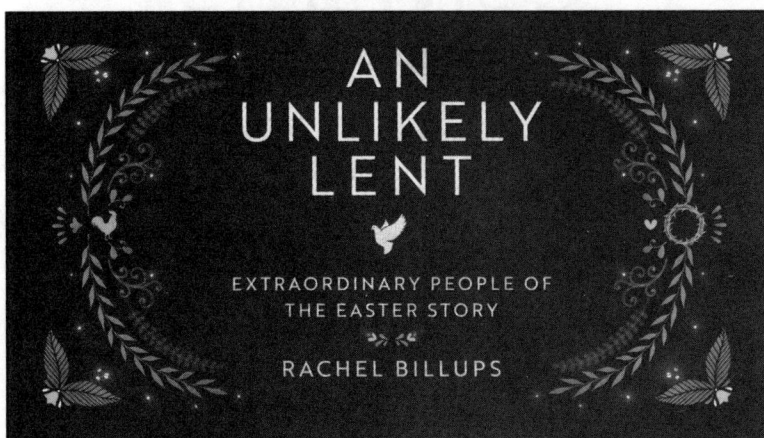

Scan the QR code below or visit
https://bit.ly/anunlikelylent.

INTRODUCTION

I love to sing. Although I am not particularly gifted in vocal performance, I make an enthusiastic choir member. There's something about lifting my voice with others, blending in harmonies, and feeling the music resonate deep in my soul. So when I was asked to participate in an ecumenical Easter cantata, I readily agreed. The local Church of God would be hosting this grand event, and my future mother-in-law happened to be the choir director. I wanted to be part of something meaningful, something that told the greatest story ever known in a way that reached people beyond mere words.

The choir practiced for months. But more than music, there was a theatrical aspect to the cantata. Many local craftsmen and craftswomen created a realistic tomb, a Roman road, and even a rugged wooden cross. Long before the days of Amazon and mass production, costumes were lovingly handmade. My boyfriend at the time reveled in his role as a Roman soldier. His older brother was portraying Jesus, and they both took their roles seriously. There was a moment in the play when the Roman soldier was supposed to strike Jesus before leading him to the cross. "I want you to hit me with force," his older brother insisted. You can imagine my boyfriend was happy to comply.

Introduction

That moment disturbed me. Even though it was just a reenactment, it felt raw, too real. Why is it that we fixate so much on the brutality of the Crucifixion? Why do we linger in the suffering, almost relishing the gruesomeness of the punishment? We speak of the pain, the nails, the crown of thorns. We hear of the Roman soldiers and the key players, folks like Pontius Pilate, Peter, and Judas. But what about everyone else? The ones watching, grieving, wondering? What about those who don't hold the central roles but whose stories still matter?

The story of Easter is rightfully centered on the crucifixion and resurrection of Jesus. But the Resurrection was not witnessed in isolation; it unfolded before a crowd. In that crowd were women and men who slipped through the margins of our Bibles, people who stood in the shadows but whose presence still shaped the moment. Might their stories have something to teach us today? There was the servant girl who confronted Peter. Or the story of Simon of Cyrene who was just minding his own business when he was compelled to carry Jesus's cross. May we find in them an invitation to a different kind of Lenten journey—a journey that explores freedom, courage, and connection through the lives of these unlikely characters. As we embark on this forty-day journey, may we discover a new dimension of God's pervading love and a fresh resurrection experience for our own lives.

In chapter 1 we begin in Bethany at the home of Jesus's closest friends. Mary of Bethany's story is one of extravagant devotion and an excessive offering. In a society where women were often relegated to the sidelines, Mary steps forward with a bold and lavish act of divine adoration. She anoints Jesus's feet with a costly perfume, an act that demonstrates her deep love for Jesus while foreshadowing his impending death and burial. This act raises the question: are we prepared to defy the norms of the day and offer Jesus our unlikely offerings?

As we continue our journey, in chapter 2 we encounter the servant girl whose words present Peter with an unlikely opposition. Peter follows Jesus at a notable distance after his arrest. It is not a high priest or a Roman official who first calls him out but a servant girl, a young woman, nameless and seemingly insignificant. She sees Peter and boldly claims, "You were with him." Peter, caught off guard, denies it. And so begins his unraveling. But what if the servant girl is not just an accuser? What if she is a mirror? What if she forces Peter, and by extension you and me, to look deeper, to confront what is stirring inside? Sometimes the challenges that unsettle us are the very ones that transform us. This girl, often overlooked in the narrative, becomes the catalyst for Peter's internal reckoning, and in her we find an invitation to examine our own experiences of opposition.

In chapter 3 we find Barabbas. Barabbas's release represents an unlikely freedom. He is the man chosen by the crowd to be released instead of Jesus. Barabbas is often painted as a villain, a man unworthy of mercy. But what if we've misunderstood his story? What if his release, as unfair as it seemed, reflects the irresistible grace of God? Might there be places in our own lives where we still cling to the shame we've experienced in our lives? Are there parts of our story that still need to experience the scandalous, unearned, and unfair love of God? Barabbas reminds us that God's grace often defies our logic, extending freedom to those we deem undeserving, just as it does to us.

In chapter 4 we walk alongside Simon of Cyrene, who reminds us of the importance of an unlikely companionship. He did not wake up that day expecting to carry a cross. He was an outsider just passing by and was pulled into the unfolding drama of redemption. Compelled to carry Jesus's cross, he became part of the story. This reminds us that even Jesus did not walk the road to the cross alone. He needed human help. Why do we resist help when we need it most? Why do we act as if faith is a solo journey when the very heart of the gospel is community? What if we embraced an interdependent faith, one where we bear one another's burdens? Simon's story calls us to rethink how we respond when we are pulled into the suffering of others. Will we resist, or will we step into the role God places before us?

Among the most powerful figures at the cross are the women who remained by Jesus's side, exhibiting in chapter 5 an unlikely courage. The women at the cross stayed when others fled. These women did not turn away from the suffering. They remained, watching, witnessing, and grieving. Their presence was an act of profound bravery. What does it mean to show up and stand by someone when the world falls apart? What are the possibilities of presence in the face of fear? Who are we being called to stand beside today? These women teach us that courage is not always loud or forceful; sometimes, it is simply the act of staying, bearing witness, and refusing to abandon those in need.

And finally in chapter 6, we come to Joseph of Arimathea and Nicodemus, two men who demonstrate an unlikely alliance. These were men of power and privilege, yet they risked everything to care for Jesus's body. They stepped forward when it mattered most, using their influence to ensure Jesus was entombed with dignity. Their actions challenge us to rethink power, to reconsider how we use our resources for God's kingdom. Where is God calling us to be unlikely allies? Who needs us to step forward, to offer our time, influence, or resources in a way that furthers love and justice? Their willingness to show up when others had abandoned Jesus reminds us that faithfulness often requires us to step beyond our comfort zones and align ourselves with God's purposes, even when it carries a cost.

This is an unlikely Lent, a season not just of giving up, but of stepping into the unfolding story of Easter—a practice in seeing what has been overlooked; an experience of meeting Jesus, not just in the grand moments, but in the in-between: in the silence, in the side characters, and in the questions.

And as we journey with these unlikely men and women, as we step into their stories, we may just discover that the Resurrection is not just a past event. The Resurrection is an invitation into something new; something unexpected; something unlikely. With each chapter you will experience personal reflection, biblical content as well as an invitation into a Lenten practice. I encourage you to participate in the weekly practices, either individually, in small group, or within worship.

So come, let us take this journey together. Let us be open to surprise. Let us embrace the discomfort of new perspectives, the beauty of hidden moments, the power of presence, of grace, and of connection. Let us walk through this season with eyes wide open, ready to see where God is moving, even in the margins. Since the cross is not the end of the story, let us embrace every unlikely moment along the way.

Chapter 1
UNLIKELY OFFERING
Mary of Bethany

Mary took a pound of costly perfume made of pure nard, anointed Jesus's feet, and wiped them with her hair. The house was filled with the fragrance of the perfume.

John 12:3

Together we are stepping into the season of the traditional church calendar known as Lent. Lent is a season I have grown to love and appreciate for its fresh invitation to life and its reflection on suffering and death. It's a forty-day journey when many people will choose to engage in particular spiritual practices. Some may choose to give up habits that seem to distract or block our connection to God. Still others will embrace practices that are centering and life-giving to ourselves and those around us.

Whether we are laying down distractions or picking up new possibilities, these forty days invite us to reengage with Jesus's life, death on the cross, and ultimately the resurrection of Easter. Lent is essentially a season of preparation and together we are exploring women and men, characters in the Gospel accounts, who participate in the events leading up to Jesus's crucifixion; but these very real humans seldom take center stage. They do not make their way into our Palm Sunday cantata, or an Easter play complete with costume-covered Roman soldiers. The story of Easter is generally focused on the crucifixion and resurrection of Jesus with a few key players. Peter, John, Mary Magdalene, just to name a few, are the focus of many messages and Bible studies. But I am curious: what else was happening around that earth-shattering event and whom did it involve? Perhaps women and men who seemed to slip through the margins of our Bibles? Might a curious exploration of their stories have something to teach us today? Could we together experience God once again in the unlikely? Today we begin around the table.

Food Offerings

Have you ever found yourself in a situation where you just wanted to do something to help? Perhaps you experienced a neighbor, a coworker, or a friend who lost someone they love and you wanted to do something, anything, to demonstrate your care and mindfulness. Maybe you decided to send a text. Some who enjoy talking may make a phone call. And if you are so inclined, you might even decide to bring food, have a meal delivered, or bake a fresh loaf of bread as a sign of your compassion. These acts of love and compassion are never about the casserole. A food offering is our excuse to connect human to human. Food is a tangible sign of love declaring I see you, I love you, and I am here to help.

Louise Butts always made the most delicious food. She was my mom's friend. And now that I think about it, I realize she was my mom's best friend. Kids do not expect their parents to have best friends and certainly they were not the paint-your-nails-on-a-Friday-night besties. My mom, Linda, and Louise were not even let's-go-on-a-girl-trip buds. They were the kind of best friends who knew the struggles within your family, your parenting woes, and your money shortages. They were committed to walking out life's journey together.

While I was growing up, Louise and my mom took turns picking up Louise's daughter, Caressa, and me from track practice. I secretly loved when Louise picked us up because it usually meant I would spend a few extra minutes at her house for what I affectionately called "first dinner." Louise's idea of an after-school snack was a delicious soup, homemade bread, and a decadent dessert. Would we be having her gooey cinnamon-soaked monkey bread? She had perfected the art of making chocolate no-bake cookies. Louise's no-bakes were my absolute favorite. There was something about the way she laid out the bowls, the spoons, even the butter for our bread. Each gesture seemed chock-full of love. I remember dreaming that someday I would be that kind of momma when I grew into adulthood. News flash, I am not that kind of momma; ain't nobody got time to be that kind of momma. But I must tell you that when my mom's cancer journey brought her home with hospice, this same woman showed up with pots of food and pies in hand.

Determined to die at home, my mom wanted to be surrounded by friends, family, and the land that she loved. There's something centering about belonging to the land. Even though she said she wasn't going to plant a garden that year, she did. Of course it was smaller, but she grew the fruits and vegetables she loved: string beans, ripe red strawberries, mouthwatering sweet potatoes, and zucchini as big as your arm! My mom and dad had worked our family farm for over forty years, and just driving onto the property after numerous hospital stays seemed to relax my mom. She seemed as if she could breathe again. As she rested in her hospice bed, her smile indicated that being home felt just right. She went home to be on the farm, to be surrounded by family and friends. And I was not sure she would get what she wanted: to be surrounded by the people she loved. But people just kept coming: church people, family people, and friend people. Louise came every day with chicken and noodles, mashed potatoes, her homemade spaghetti, fresh-baked bread and pies. Oh my goodness the pies. There was nearly a pie for every member of my family: cherry pies, coconut cream pies, apple pies, pumpkin pies, and pecan pies. So many pies! We had to insist that everyone who visited my mom eat a piece of pie. My dad, brother, sister, and I could not consume the carbs fast enough. The pies were broken and shared with everyone who stopped by to chat, to sing, to pray, to cry, to grieve, and to celebrate. Food was the offering. It was a little over the top, it was extravagant, and it made the human connection so rich.

Perhaps you, too, have experienced food offerings. Maybe when one of your loved ones walked through the valley of the shadow of death, someone brought food. Or possibly when there's been much to celebrate, a person or group of people came with an offering. It's the casserole that shows up when a child is born, the cinnamon rolls shared among teachers on the last day of school, your best friend who invites you to dinner when you receive a promotion, and even the zucchini bread shared by a neighbor just because they baked an extra loaf. But food offerings are never really about the menu items. Food offerings are always about our deeply human connection, and it's been that way for a long, long time. Beyond the twelve disciples, Mary, Martha, and Lazarus were Jesus's closest best friends. It was unclear as to why this trio held such a tender place in Jesus's heart, but it's not hard to imagine that Jesus enjoyed numerous nights in their home, and more meals around their table than they could count. Jesus gathered with his best friends for a meal in the Gospel of John to celebrate, because as we all know, tomorrow is not promised.

Tomorrow Is Not Promised

In John's Gospel Jesus has just raised Lazarus from the dead. And Lazarus had been dead for a while. So dead that the sisters were worried that when those milling about helped open his grave, Lazarus was going to smell terribly bad. Initially his body had been prepped, anointed, and wrapped for the long slumber and yet Jesus's "Lazarus, come out" called him back to life on this side of heaven. Of course that's a colossal reason to celebrate, but not too much too fast because Jesus already knew he was in trouble. Jesus once again created a disturbance among the naysayers, so much so that they were ready to eradicate him and his traveling ministry. Jesus took a risk coming to Bethany to heal his friend, and now he's together with them once again in that same small town. There was an urgency as John wrote about this gathering. I encourage you to read the Gospel of John 11 and 12 together. When you do read those chapters, you will pick up on a tension in the text that seems so thick you can nearly taste it. We are no strangers to tension. I imagine most have experienced tension around tables. At that family gathering where your uncle goes into a political tirade, you experience tension. The wayward cousin decides to show up at the last minute to everyone's surprise, and suddenly there is tension. The work party where someone did not realize a coworker has been let go for not-great reasons, and they inquire, "Where's Sam?"—you've got tension! The air is thick, the conversation minimal, and those in the room don't know exactly what to do or say. It's this kind of tension that I imagine the disciples were experiencing around Lazarus, Martha, and Mary's dinner table:

> *Six days before the Passover Jesus came to Bethany, the home of Lazarus, whom he had raised from the dead. There they gave a dinner for him. Martha served, and Lazarus was one of those reclining with him. Mary took a pound of costly perfume made of pure nard, anointed Jesus's feet, and wiped them with her hair. The house was filled with the fragrance of the perfume.*
>
> John 12:1-3

John situated the reader at the table, preparing for the defining meal of the Jewish faith known as the Passover. The Passover was less than a week away and like a master storyteller John's just building the tension. Imagine the scene with me: Jesus and the disciples are reclining at the home of Lazarus, and Martha was serving. Again, not a surprise: according to the writer of Luke, Martha was in the habit of doing such things:

> *Now as they went on their way, he [Jesus] entered a certain village where a woman named Martha welcomed him. She had*

a sister named Mary, who sat at Jesus's feet and listened to what
he was saying.

Luke 10:38-39

Martha was not particularly happy with her younger sister, Mary, for not aiding in the preparations. Is this the same Mary and Martha story with a different twist? Is the writer of the Gospel of John attempting to give us a different angle? It's not exactly clear. But what is clear is that Mary decided to offer Jesus an extravagant gift. Mary, sitting at Jesus's feet as was her habit is our sign that Mary, too, was a disciple and a student of Jesus. But on this occasion Mary was not merely listening. She had brought with her a gift and an intention to share it. As Jesus was speaking, she gently lifted a pound of costly nard perfume out of her bag and anointed Jesus's feet with that oil. The word for anointed, *ēleipsen*, is the same word used when talking about preparing a body for burial. Mary anointed Jesus's feet and then wiped those same feet with her hair. Her action certainly did not dissipate the tension. These actions added to it. Here's a woman, a follower and friend of Jesus who touched Jesus's feet, letting down her hair. There was an intimacy to her actions. Mary did not seem to act in desperation, but rather shamelessly poured out an extravagant offering onto Jesus. I wonder, did the disciples look away, did her actions leave them speechless? There were no immediate protests as Mary focused on washing her friend's feet.

But why would Mary do such a thing? Was this a sign that she was just so grateful for Jesus's healing her brother? Did she not know what else to do? Jesus will later say she bought the perfume. But how did she buy this perfume and with what? Were Mary and her sister, Martha, independently wealthy? Did Mary own some sort of small business? Could this nard have been part of her inheritance? Was this woman literally pouring her dowry over Jesus's feet as a sign of her unrivaled commitment to Jesus and his ministry? Burn the ships, pour out your most prized possession, Mary! Mary seemed to be with Jesus no matter what. She seemed to be giving Jesus her all.

Sometimes this is when I wish I could be a participant around that table. While Mary anointed Jesus's feet, did the men nervously laugh, did they groan in protest, did some even applaud Mary? We don't know. Perhaps everyone around the room was merely stunned. There's also this assumption that Jesus was always traveling with a posse. Was it merely the twelve or were there more? Were men and women seated together? Were there children to witness this exchange?

I feel compelled to give Judas a bit of credit. While the room full of dinner guests were watching this alternative ritual in shock and horror, Judas asked perhaps what others were wondering:

> *"Why was this perfume not sold for three hundred denarii and the money given to the poor?"*
>
> *John 12:5*

The author of John added a little commentary, stating that Judas did not actually care about the poor and used to steal money from the common purse. Really? That conclusion seems a bit suspect because wouldn't the disciples just deem Judas irresponsible and keep the purse themselves? Or at the very least, I imagine the disciples asking Jesus to rebuke Judas for his robbing them all. Maybe the author added this bit of commentary because he needed to suggest a reason that Judas would later betray Jesus.

Since it was nearly unthinkable, he needed to justify Judas's later behavior.

Sometimes we have relationships, friendships, partnerships that go south and it's only in hindsight we realize that something underneath the surface was going on. At times we attempt to justify why we did not see the infringement in the moment: the affair, the embezzlement, the betrayal, and so we say things like, *he or she was always shady*, but that was not really the case. Humans can be really human, meaning that sometimes people get caught up in making bad choices. And sometimes people, particularly us religious types, attempt to portray ourselves beyond our human condition. We say things to ourselves like, *I would never do that; I would never say that; there is just no way I could get caught up in something so suspect.* But I've been around long enough to realize we all are capable of making less than great choices for ourselves and others.

Yes, Judas was only human after all. But Jesus was not having it with Judas that day:

> *"Leave her alone. She bought it so that she might keep it for the day of my burial. You always have the poor with you, but you do not always have me."*
>
> John 12:7-8

Jesus responded to his anointer's critics tagging an Old Testament scripture, Deuteronomy 15:11, "Since there will never cease to be some in need on the earth, I therefore command you, 'Open your hand to the poor and needy neighbor in your land.'" I've experienced too many people in ministry use John 12:7-8, as justification for not caring for the poor. They place words, these words, in Jesus's mouth as a mere mandate to ignore the vulnerable among us with sometimes political implications. But the hearers in the room would have heard the depth of this scripture. The Old Testament was always encouraging (dare I say challenging) the faithful to care for the foreigner, the widow, and the orphan among us. Jesus had a deep passion for caring for the vulnerable. Judas could have been portraying some kind of false piety, and maybe Jesus called him out for his future mishaps. Or maybe Judas was merely the target because Jesus understood the discomfort of the witnesses in the room. Even I struggle to imagine Jesus this vulnerable: a Jesus who needed to be prepared for burial. Mary's gift to Jesus eased the tension in his body as he made his way toward Jerusalem. A needy Jesus does not seem to align with the Jesus of the Gospel of John. And no matter the interpretation of this exchange between Judas and Jesus, Jesus was opening the door for there to be more ways than one to offer love, to bless others, to honor the divine.

Grace on the Menu

I am always surprised by Jesus's treatment of women throughout the Gospels. Jesus's interactions with women were revolutionary and deeply personal. Take John 4, for example, where Jesus met the Samaritan woman at the well. Not only did he break cultural and gender norms by speaking to this woman, but he invited her into a deep theological conversation about worship and the living water that Jesus could provide. This was unheard of in the first century. Rabbis did not engage with women like this, much less Samaritan women. Yet Jesus did not just talk to her; he saw her, valued her, and gave her the dignity of understanding. And her response? She ran back to her village, becoming one of the first true evangelists, sharing the good news of Jesus with her people.

Another surprise encounter was with the woman caught in adultery in John 8. This Gospel of John story was loaded with possibilities for entrapment from the beginning. The religious leaders brought a woman to Jesus, hoping to pin him down in some theological or legal mistake. But Jesus, in his brilliance, refused to play their game and instead turned the spotlight on the accusers, confronting their own sinfulness. And then when the crowd dispersed, Jesus did not shame the woman. Jesus did not condemn her, but instead extended a pathway of grace, saying, "Go now and leave your life of sin." Jesus offered her a future, a second chance, a path to freedom. Again, we see Jesus lifting a woman out of shame and offering her dignity and grace.

So now here's Mary of Bethany, anointing Jesus with expensive perfume and the criticism is on! The disciples, especially Judas, were ready to write her off for her extravagance. But Jesus protected her, even praised her, saying, "Leave her alone." Her offering, misunderstood by others, was honored by Jesus. There are other accounts in the Gospel of this type of anointing.

Jesus sat in Bethany at the house of Simon, but this time the woman was unnamed:

> While he was at Bethany in the house of Simon the leper, as he sat at the table, a woman came with an alabaster jar of very costly ointment of nard, and she broke open the jar and poured the ointment on his head.
>
> Mark 14:3

Or even in Luke's Gospel, there is a different Simon, a different location, and most likely a very different woman.

*One of the Pharisees asked Jesus to eat with him, and when he
went into the Pharisee's house he reclined to dine. And a woman
in the city who was a sinner, having learned that he was eating
in the Pharisee's house, brought an alabaster jar of ointment.
She stood behind him at his feet, weeping, and began to bathe
his feet with her tears and to dry them with her hair, kissing his
feet and anointing them with the ointment.*

Luke 7:36-38

The similarities are obvious: there's the anointing, the hair,
the offering poured out over Jesus. But the differences are also
glaring: the names, the locations, the vocations of these women.
And yet in every account, Jesus defended the women, when the
men folk around were so quick to dismiss the actions of these
women. Grace was always on the menu when Jesus interacted
with women. John's Gospel seemed to kind of smoosh these
stories of the women together with Mary representing them all in
a profound and prophetic way.

Who is this Mary of Bethany anyway? For years scholars have
chastised the storytellers of the early churches for their tendency
to meld all of its female identities together: the good, the bad,
and the in-between. And although I do not like to assume that
everyone who touched Jesus's feet had some kind of scandalous
past, there is helpful insight in the theory that purports that these
women were all indeed one disciple.

Last spring I found myself listening to Diana Butler Bass at
a gathering of leaders and innovators with the Texas Methodist
Foundation talk about scholarship surrounding Mary and
Martha and early manuscripts that did not include Martha within
the stories. Butler Bass referenced the scholarship of Elizabeth
Schrader Polczer and her *Resurrecting Mary the Tower*, where she

questions whether or not the Mary of Bethany was in fact Mary Madgalene prior to scribes shifting the name Mary to Martha. In an interview with Peter Enns, Polczer explained, "One in five Greek manuscripts has a problem around Martha, and one in three old Latin manuscripts has a problem around Martha. So, it's really happening throughout the entire textual transmission."[1]

I was fascinated. What if this textual problem was created to downplay Mary's role in Jesus's life? Maybe Mary was not one of the Twelve, but nonetheless, she was one who understood Jesus's power and purpose far better than the men witnessing her actions. This feet-anointing Mary emerged as a passionate follower of Jesus, preparing his body for his ultimate death and burial. And isn't that just like history? Time and time again, we see how powerful women, devoted disciples, and fierce followers of Jesus get pushed to the margins. We take their names and shift them, adjust their stories, and rewrite their contributions. But what if Mary was more than just a background character? What if she was the disciple who saw Jesus with more clarity than anyone else? While Peter was busy denying, and Thomas was caught in doubt, Mary was right there—fully present, fully aware, and fully engaged in the deep mystery of Christ's purpose. She was not waiting for permission to believe. Mary simply knew.

Imagine the radical implications of this theory: a woman, often overlooked, was the one preparing Jesus for the greatest moment in history. She did not wield power the way the world expects. Mary did not have a title or a position among the Twelve, but her actions declared a devotion that was tangible and real. Maybe we've missed something by pushing Mary's story aside. Maybe, in recovering her rightful place, we see a clearer picture of what true discipleship looks like. True discipleship with Mary looked like deep devotion, bold action, and an unwavering love for Jesus that refuses to be erased. She poured herself out in that offering.

The Offering

The offering was spikenard imported most likely from a region in what is now India. It's an expensive offering valued at three hundred denarii. A denarius was a common worker's daily wage. We are talking minimum wage, but still worth an entire year's salary. That's a lot of money for a traveling group of people living off the generosity of others. So it's no wonder Judas protested! And then there was the smell! Pure nard imported from the mountains of India, was purposed to be used sparingly to mask the odors of everyday life. What happens when a person takes an entire pound of pure nard and pours it out on Jesus's feet? It starts to spill into the rug, splashing on the linens covering the table. The aroma filled the nostrils of everyone in the room. The scent would have been overwhelming.

I'll never forget smelling that anointing oil. I was standing on the slippery floor of a YMCA in Greenville, Ohio. Its pool was our strategy for baptizing people by immersion. Tom had already been baptized as a baby, but sometimes it is difficult for people to understand United Methodist theology surrounding baptism. Yes, United Methodist clergy baptize babies but we do not baptize infants to secure their eternal salvation. It's not about that, but clergy also do not rebaptize people because we firmly believe that God is the actor in baptism. And what God did once, God does not need to do again. Tom was adamant, however. He wanted to publicly declare his faith through baptism, and did I mention I was a provisional elder in The United Methodist Church at the time and not yet ordained? I had a deep ethical vein and would not allow myself to do something I was not permitted to do. But Tom persisted. "Rachel, can't you do something?" he asked emphatically. I thought about his request for quite some time. "Well, Tom, perhaps I could anoint you with oil as a sign of the work you've felt God doing in your life." I'm not sure to this day why I decided to use oil. Truth be told I haven't used anointing oil for anything but prayers of healing since Tom's anointing. So I traveled to a local pottery shop and purchased a jar that looked somewhat old and rugged and then purchased the biggest batch of anointing oil I could find. The oil was scented with Rose of Sharon. I now recognize that I could have merely used some olive oil and supplemented with a few tiny jars of the scented stuff, but I didn't.

The day came for Tom's anointing, and there were other people prepared for immersion baptism. Men, women, and teens were waiting to be immersed that day, but we started with Tom's public declaration of faith. He looked at me, grinning from ear to ear. And I asked, "Why are you here today, Tom?" There were nearly fifty people gathered to hear Tom's poolside testimony. I cannot recall exactly what he said, but he wanted people to know he was committed to following Jesus. I prayed over him and poured the oil over his head, probably an entire cup of anointing oil with a smell that was so strong it made my eyes water. The Rose of Sharon was strong! And there was no way Tom was ever getting that smell out of the clothes he was wearing. In the holiness of the moment, everyone gathered, encircled Tom, and placed hands on him to pray. With each touch, oil was exchanged, and no one was getting out of that YMCA without the fragrance of the anointing oil on their person. We cheered Tom on for stepping into this new season of faith. Tom was beaming and my integrity was left intact. Several months later, after I left that church to serve at a new congregation, I received the call that Tom had died suddenly of a massive heart attack at the age of forty-six.

I still have that jar and although it no longer holds oil, to this day it smells unmistakably like Rose of Sharon. Every time I hold the jar I think of Tom and feel immensely grateful that we were able to use an unlikely offering to create memorable space for him to publicly declare his faith. And every time I read of a story of anointing in the Bible, I can't help thinking of Tom's commitment to following Jesus. So I wonder, what about you? Maybe you've never experienced an anointing in church? Maybe you can't even imagine the overwhelming aroma, but each one of us has gifts to offer Jesus and one another.

An Unlikely Offering

I am a sucker for internet videos that catch people in a random act of kindness. You scroll to a video where a woman in the checkout line pays for someone's groceries, a man buys an extra sandwich for a hungry traveler, a stranger on the street asks a passerby for extra change to pay for parking and his need is met.

Usually, the requests are minimal. The ask is simple and easy, and yet many times people are in too big of a hurry to meet the needs presented by the person filming. I can't be too harsh. Maybe they do not meet the request because they do not have the extra cash. Or perhaps those who pass by are already behind schedule. I certainly can think of numerous times that I've just ignored someone or something around me because I had people to see and places to be. I did not have time to be inconvenienced by people.

But then someone does give the extra couple of bucks, pays the parking, buys the cup of coffee, and suddenly the receiver becomes the giver. They hand the person $1,000 cash. Usually this is when the woman or man is brought to tears. They begin sharing a piece of their story: there are bills to pay, mouths to feed, a car that just broke down, and an uncertainty on how to arrive at any solution. Sometimes the story goes deeper, however; the internet does its thing and before we know it a total stranger has a new car, medical debt that has been paid, and a refurbished apartment is in the works. It's extravagant, it's over the top, it's for one person, and the extravagant generosity is beautiful. In a world where scarcity seems to be the name of the game, abundance feels like a healing balm. Perhaps that was Jesus's point: this unlikely offering was over the top; a demonstration of the grace God was pouring over all of creation. What I love most about the character of God is that God chose not to do this work alone, but rather, now we have the opportunity to experience God's abundance on earth as it is in heaven. We can offer God and others over-the-top generosity.

I am struck by how Mary offered her very best to Jesus, an unlikely gift of costly perfume that completely filled the room with the fragrance of her love and devotion. It was not practical, it was not expected, but oh my, the offering was beautiful. And it makes me wonder: what does that look like among us now? What is your unlikely offering? Maybe you don't have the mad skill of making pies to share with your dying best friend, but what about using your creativity, your expertise, or your passions in unexpected ways to bless the world?

Imagine a graphic designer offering free branding to a struggling small business, or a retired teacher tutoring kids in their neighborhood who can't afford extra help. Maybe you're a barber who could spend an afternoon cutting hair for people experiencing homelessness, or a photographer capturing portraits for foster families who might not have the means to have professional photos taken. What about someone who has a knack for listening, really listening, offering their time to sit with someone who feels invisible? I am in awe of the care and calling team at New Albany United Methodist Church: twenty laypersons who give of their time to visit and listen to the most vulnerable adults among us. Many times, these adults lack mobility; they cannot attend church, but these persons bring the church to them. And they pour out words of love and grace over those who are homebound. These acts may seem small, but they reflect a love that's both surprising and potentially transformative.

The beauty of an unlikely offering is that it catches the world off guard. It does not follow the rules of efficiency or practicality; rather, an unlikely offering comes from within. Think of the nurse who stays late to comfort a patient who is struggling to make sense of this new health crisis, the mechanic who volunteers to fix cars for single parents, or the gardener who grows fresh vegetables to share with the local food pantry. These gifts may not come with fanfare, but they carry the intoxicating fragrance of God's love into spaces so desperately in need.

I invite you to offer Jesus and the world your very best. Your unlikely offering does not have to be perfect. Perhaps your pies are not Instagram worthy. The offering does not have to make sense to everyone else. Like Mary of Bethany, your offering just has to come from a willing heart. So as we step together into the season of Lent, let's explore what our own unlikely offerings might be. What do you have in your hands, your home, your heart, that can be poured out as a gift? When we offer what we have, albeit unlikely, unexpected, and perhaps a little over the top, the aroma will be remarkable. It will catch the world off guard and the one for whom it's intended will be blessed.

Practice: The Offering

During this season of Lent, consider making space for an offering: a gift of love, devotion, or generosity that may seem unusual or unexpected but speaks deeply to Jesus. In this practice I invite both individuals and church groups to explore what you can pour out in faith. One possibility for engaging in this practice is through personal reflection and journaling. Set aside time each day this week to meditate on the question: what is my unlikely offering? Write about your skills, resources, or acts of love that may seem small or unconventional, but you could use to bless others. Perhaps it's an act of generosity that doesn't make sense to everyone but speaks volumes in the kingdom of God.

Church groups could create spaces for people to offer and receive prayer and anointing, either in a dedicated worship service or through interactive prayer stations where individuals can anoint one another. These moments of anointing can serve as a time of surrender, inviting participants to ask, Lord, what is mine to pour out? What do I have in my hands, my heart, my life that you can use to love God and others?

Another way to practice offerings is through acts of service. Individuals or groups can commit to giving their time and presence in unexpected ways, such as visiting someone who is lonely, providing a meal for a struggling family, or offering encouragement to those in need. Churches might organize a "generosity challenge," where people intentionally find creative ways to give, whether through financial gifts, time, or even simple gestures of kindness.

No offering is too small, and no act of love goes unnoticed in the kingdom of God. Whether as an individual or a community, take time this Lent to listen for God's call. Step into acts of unexpected generosity, and allow your offering, whatever it may be, to reflect God's love in the world.

God of abundance and grace, thank you for receiving our unlikely offerings, poured out in love. Teach us to give boldly, even when our gifts seem extravagant or misunderstood. Help us to recognize your presence in every act of generosity and every aroma of devotion. May our offerings fill the world with the fragrance of your love. Amen.

Chapter 2
UNLIKELY OPPOSITION
The Servant Girl

While Peter was below in the courtyard, one of the female servants of the high priest came by. When she saw Peter warming himself, she stared at him and said, "You also were with Jesus, the man from Nazareth."

Mark 14:66-67

Sometimes when I explore people in the Bible, I discover pages of research because scholars consider their contribution to the divine narrative noteworthy. And then there are people like the servant girl. Unnamed and yet vital to the tension in the Passion, especially regarding Peter, the servant girl plays a pivotal role in helping the reader understand what's at stake in Jesus's trial. As I approached this character, I began to imagine her role in a very different light and invite you to do the same. I have always understood the servant girl to be a source of opposition in Peter's life, and therefore a less-than-good player in the Passion story. Now I have come to reconsider my perspective and invite you to do the same.

I was determined to soak up some January sunshine, despite the extremely low temperatures, so I set out to explore the wonder of Old Man's Cave and Cedar Falls. Old Man's Cave and Cedar Falls are in the heart of a region called the Hocking Hills, near Logan, Ohio. Massive cave and rock formations seem to be dropped into the middle of an ever-expanding forest. Reader, it is a piece of heaven. The round-trip hike is nearly six miles, and I completely underestimated how long it would take to trek through over ten inches of snow. But let me tell you, the hike was worth every frigid step. I stood in awe of the icicles that towered above me on the edges of the cliffs. I breathed deep of the crisp, cool air and the sun that sparkled off the brilliant white snow. Although there were a few footprints in the fresh snow, I nearly felt bad for disrupting the beauty with each of my steps. Have you ever walked through deep snow? It's kind of like trekking through the sand on the beach. So by the time I made it to the halfway point, Cedar Falls, I was winded, tired, and ready to be done.

On my return trip to Old Man's Cave, I popped in an earbud and listened to Father Gregory Boyle's latest book, *Cherished Belonging*. As Father Boyle spoke about the boundless love of God, how everyone belongs to God and to one another, I could not help wanting to clap back with a resounding, "No way, Father Boyle, not everybody!" I could feel the tension rising in my body. I thought to myself, what about the people who seem bent on destruction? What about those with little regard for the most vulnerable? I am not so sure that we can categorically believe that everyone belongs, not in the world we are living in now. I know there are some people I just do not want in my circle of belonging: people who have been acting foolish on social media; people claiming so-called biblical truths that have nothing to do with the Bible. I was arguing with everyone and no one in particular while surrounded by the majesty of that winter wonderland. And, Reader, my heart grew as frosty as my surroundings. Perhaps you, too, have found yourself in similar situations. Whether that's because you've been scrolling through social media, watching your news source of choice, or attempting to make sense of the senseless world we find ourselves in; you, too, have said to everyone and no one in particular, "No way! Not everyone can possibly be in the circle of belonging."

These are tense times and intense times. And when people experience tension, humans tend to say and do things that are beyond the divine identity they have claimed for themselves. For example, sometimes I find myself asking, "Rachel, what has got a hold of you?" There have been moments I find myself posting, deleting, and nearly reposting less-than-thoughtful comments on people's social media posts. I'm tempted to be a keyboard warrior. In that moment I want to put people in their place. And somehow, I believe that I will set the world right with my words. I want to help the person who is posting understand just how wrong they are with what they have posted for the whole world to see. And then what, Rachel? Will they repent of their dubious ways and return to some form of sanity? Or am I merely attempting to make myself feel better when I do not know what else to do?

Tense Times

In tense times humans do strange things. It seems to be what was happening in the Gospel of Mark. The situation was tense; Jesus had just been arrested. He was outed by one of his own, Judas, with an intimate kiss on the cheek. The chief priests, elders, scribes, and accompanying mob arrived carrying clubs and swords. And once Jesus was in the possession of the powers that be, someone, apparently Peter, drew a sword and took off the ear of the high priest's slave. Jesus stopped the violence with his words, but the disciples ran like hell. You know it's an emergency, because the Gospel writer Mark outs himself as having to run away naked. No reasonable Jewish man is going to run naked through the streets. Running naked would be a form of social self-annihilation, and yet Mark was presumably running for his life. They all ran, refusing to be captured by the temple guards. Alone and abandoned, Jesus was led to stand trial before the Sanhedrin, led by the chief priest. Where were his disciples now? They could have been there to advocate on Jesus's behalf. The disciples had spent several years with this Jesus of Nazareth and experienced their fair share of run-ins with the religious and political powers of the day. So why run now? The times are so tense that the only perceived choice they had was to run.

It's as if we are watching a movie on a large screen and the director takes a wide-lens view, when suddenly near the edge of the screen we witness the disciple Peter watching the drama from a distance. Peter was the speak-first-think-later disciple, but if he was anything, Peter was a man of action. Peter likely believed that he needed to do something, but what? Perhaps Peter can give us a clue.

While Peter was below in the courtyard, one of the female servants of the high priest came by. When she saw Peter warming himself, she stared at him and said, "You also were with Jesus, the man from Nazareth." But he denied it, saying, "I do not know or understand what you are talking about." And he went out into the forecourt. Then the cock crowed.

Mark 14:66-72

Nobody Wants to Die

It should not surprise us that Peter, when confronted by one of the female servants of the high priest, chose self-preservation, as did all the disciples in the garden. Jesus was clearly thought to be a threat to religious stability and political peace. Jesus was to be tried as some sort of religious rebel and Peter was well aware of what happens to those who find themselves in these situations. Jesus has caught the attention of the high priest named in the Gospels of Matthew and John as Caiaphas:

Then the chief priests and the elders of the people gathered in the courtyard of the high priest, who was called Caiaphas, and they conspired to arrest Jesus by stealth and kill him.

Matthew 26:3-4

So the chief priests and the Pharisees called a meeting of the council and said, "What are we to do? This man is performing many signs. If we let him go on like this, everyone will believe in him, and the Romans will come and destroy both our holy place and our nation." But one of them, Caiaphas, who was high priest that year, said to them, "You know nothing at all!"

John 11:47-49

Caiaphas was not a high priest to be trifled with. He knew the name of the game. In a world where the Roman Empire flexed its power over every territory including Judea, Caiaphas played his role well. More than just a religious leader, Caiaphas was a political operator, keeping the fragile peace between Rome and the Jewish people. He managed to maintain Jewish religious traditions while also making sure the Temple system—its sacrifices, its offerings, and its money—kept going and flowing. More than a place of worship, the temple was an economic engine. For example, the temple tax, an annual contribution to the second temple in Jerusalem, would have cost every male above the age of twenty about two days' wages, a significant amount of money for a family in antiquity.[1] Money, grain, and sacrifices were placed and processed in and through this system. And Caiaphas was the operator of the entire enterprise. Caiaphas ensured that the temple system all ran smoothly. Caiaphas held the position and power for nearly two decades. His longevity was an impressive feat in a time when high priests came and went at Rome's whim. Caiaphas was loyal to the system. He was committed to preserving stability, but stability often comes at a cost.

And this time that cost, in Caiaphas's eyes, was Jesus. This traveling street teacher from Galilee was disrupting everything. Jesus flipped treasury tables, called out hypocrisy, and stirred up messianic hopes that could all turn dangerous. A revolution was not a mere theological debate. A revolution was a direct threat to the order Caiaphas fought to maintain. So when Jesus was arrested and dragged before him, Caiaphas was not searching for truth. Caiaphas was not interested in whether Jesus was who he said he was. Caiaphas was looking for a way to shut Jesus down. In Mark's Gospel, Jesus remained silent as the accusations piled up, silent in the face of corruption, silent in the face of power. Until Caiaphas finally asked the damning question: "Are you the Messiah, the Son of the Blessed One?" (Mark 14:61). And that's when Jesus spoke, "I am." And with those words, Jesus declares something bigger than any religious system or any political power. He claims his identity as the one who counts the stars.

With that one statement, "I am," Reader, we are taken back to Exodus and Moses's question:

> "If I come to the Israelites and say to them, 'The God of your ancestors has sent me to you,' and they ask me, 'What is his name?' what shall I say to them?" God said to Moses, "I AM WHO I AM." He said further, "Thus you shall say to the Israelites, 'I AM has sent me to you.'"
>
> *Exodus 3:13-14*

Caiaphas heard Jesus's claim to be one with God and tore his clothes in protest. Jesus was more than a dangerous rebel in Caiaphas's eyes; he was claiming to be the Son of God.

Meanwhile, just outside, Peter was warming himself by the fire. Close enough to hear, close enough to see, but not close enough to stand with Jesus. Imagining the scene is almost too much to take in. Inside Caiaphas's house, Jesus was expressing and embracing the truth of who he is, and outside, Peter, his closest disciple, was denying him, determined not to lose his own life.

When we were traveling to the Holy Land, our small group decided to make our way to the Church of St. Peter in Gallicantu. There are roosters everywhere. I cannot help smiling when I see a picture of a rooster. My uncle Mick was obsessed with roosters and chickens. My little sister and I nearly had one tattooed on our bodies, but we came to our senses. When we stepped into what was thought to be the courtyard, I noticed it, a sculpture of Peter, a Roman soldier, the servant girls (two girls in the sculpture), and a rooster. I've always been drawn to this story and somehow standing in what would have been the vicinity of that courtyard made me nearly emotional. Could I smell fires burning in the distance? What would this have looked like at night? There was no way that Peter was thinking clearly. Motivated by gut reactions, Peter had the courage to follow, to be nearly present for Jesus. It's just that when he came face-to-face with opposition, Peter seemed to cave. Peter did not want to die!

Self-preservation is an extremely human response. We witness this kind of action from the beginning of the story of God's people. First Abraham, when threated by Pharaoh, determined to pretend his wife was his sister. It was horrific and potentially jeopardized his wife's safety. I struggle with this practice. Although I understand his need for self-preservation, I cannot fathom this at the expense of his wife:

> *Now there was a famine in the land, and Abram went down to Egypt to live there for a while because the famine was severe. As he was about to enter Egypt, he said to his wife Sarai, "I know what a beautiful woman you are. When the Egyptians see you, they will say, 'This is his wife.' Then they will kill me but will let you live. Say you are my sister, so that I will be treated well for your sake and my life will be spared because of you."*
>
> *Genesis 12:10-13 NIV*

The practice did not cease with Abraham. His son Isaac did the same with his wife, Rebekah, only this time the leader was Abimelek, king of the Philistines:

> *When the men of that place asked him about his wife, he said, "She is my sister," because he was afraid to say, "She is my wife."*

He thought, "The men of this place might kill me on account of Rebekah, because she is beautiful."

Genesis 26:7 NIV

In each case these women seemed protected by God's presence even in the middle of a disturbing situation. These Old Testament patriarchs were attempting to stay alive, even if it meant harm to the women who'd held the promise of God in their wombs.

Most humans tend to self-preserve. I remember my seventh grade algebra class. I was a disruptive student. Yours truly was quite the talker. I know you are shocked. But I was never blamed for my disruptions. There was another girl in the class, my bestie, known for her troublemaking ways. The teacher always called her out for my disruptions. At first, I was relieved; I could not believe my good fortune. I thought I had gotten away with it. But after several weeks of the teacher misconstruing the situation, I couldn't take the guilt. I confessed to my math teacher, "I am the disrupter, not my best friend!" Mr. Math Teacher was not angry with me but rather commended me for my honesty. And he continued to punish my bestie even though she was innocent.

People get blamed for stuff they do not do. They are reprimanded for acts they do not commit. And sometimes humans just kind of let that go. We are just bent toward self-preservation. Think about it. It's when the car behind us gets pulled over even though we have both been speeding. It's that time when your sibling took the blame for the cookies that turned up missing. Or maybe even when coworkers get reprimanded for the mess you have made in the break room microwave. In those moments, it is easy to stay silent. Just count your lucky stars and keep your mouth shut. But what about when the stakes are higher? When people remain silent in the face of injustice, they contribute to a culture of complicity that allows harm to persist. Consider the colleague who misused the corporate credit card for personal expenses. Perhaps others in the office notice but choose to look the other way. They fear professional consequences or simply assume it is not their place to intervene. What about the moment a friend's child shows signs of abuse—bruises hidden beneath sleeves, a fearful demeanor, or troubling stories that do not add up?

People might hesitate to speak out, uncertain of the full picture or worried about the repercussions of getting involved. This silence extends beyond personal relationships into the political sphere, where people often refrain from challenging policies that harm marginalized communities, whether through systemic racism, economic exploitation, or restrictive laws that strip individuals of their rights. Whether motivated by fear, indifference, or self-preservation, remaining silent in these moments not only enables harm but also makes bystanders complicit in injustice. Our temptation is just to live our lives, do our jobs, and keep our heads down. We don't want to take the risk. That's Peter. And even though we have speculations concerning where the other eleven disciples might be, here's Peter warming himself by that fire, being defensive, quick to correct any opposition to his self-preservation:

> When [the servant girl] saw Peter warming himself, she stared at him and said, "You also were with Jesus, the man from Nazareth." But he denied it, saying, "I do not know or understand what you are talking about." And he went out into the forecourt. Then the cock crowed. And the female servant, on seeing him, began again to say to the bystanders, "This man is one of them." But again he denied it.
>
> Mark 14:67-70a

Peter is in a real pickle! Someone has confronted him with his very own identity. Peter, you are a follower of this Jesus of Nazareth. But who is this person who confronted Peter? So often I have assumed that she was merely an instrument of the temple. The servant girl was an extension of Caiaphas and his agenda. But what if we reconsidered the role this servant girl played not only in Peter's life but also in ours? Could it be that this woman wanted Peter to take a risk? Not to humiliate Peter, but rather to smoke the rebel Peter out. Did the servant girl urge him to rise to his fullest potential as an advocate of Jesus?

Worth the Risk

Very little is known about the servant girl of the high priest. Certainly, she had a function in the temple system. As a woman, she was already located on a lower tier of the socioeconomic status, and as a female servant, she was near the bottom. As F. Scott Spencer observes, "Within the prevailing patriarchal hierarchical structure of the first century Mediterranean household, servant-girls would clearly rank at the bottom of the ladder, subordinated by their gender and age as well as their slave class."[2]

Slavery was an integral part of first-century life in the early Christian community, deeply embedded in the economic, social, and domestic structures of the Roman Empire. According to scholars like N. T. Wright and Michael Byrd, slaves made up nearly 30 percent of the population in urban areas, serving in a wide range of roles that were essential to society.[3] People became slaves through various means. Some slaves were prisoners of war, others were kidnapped by traders, and many were born into slavery. In some cases, individuals voluntarily sold themselves or their family members into slavery as a means of survival, particularly during times of economic hardship. Unlike the racialized chattel slavery that defined the eighteenth and nineteenth centuries in the United States of America, Roman slavery was not tied to a single ethnicity or race. Instead, it was a widespread institution affecting people from all backgrounds, often seen as a temporary condition rather than a lifelong, inherited status.

Slaves in the Roman world performed a diverse range of tasks depending on their skills, education, and the needs of their masters. Some worked in grueling conditions as laborers in fields, mines, and workshops, while others held positions of greater responsibility and even expertise. Midwives and nurses tended to households and communities, painters and sculptors contributed to the artistic landscape, and cooks prepared elaborate meals for wealthy Roman families. Some slaves served as caretakers for children, forming close bonds with the families they served. Others worked as doctors, tutors, or accountants, roles that required advanced education and training. However, many also found themselves in more degrading positions, such as prostitution, which was a common form of exploitation for enslaved women. A slave's status and quality of life depended largely on the disposition of their master. Some were treated well and even entrusted with significant authority, while others faced harsh punishments and severe abuse.

The process of gaining freedom in the Roman world was markedly different from the American chattel slavery system. Slaves in the first century could be freed (this was called manumission) through various legal and social mechanisms. Some were granted their freedom as a reward for years of loyal service, while others were able to purchase their freedom if they had earned money through their labor. Manumission was often a public affair, involving formal ceremonies or legal declarations, and freed slaves could sometimes acquire Roman citizenship. Even after gaining their freedom, former slaves often maintained a connection with their former master, continuing to work for them or serving as a client in a patronage relationship. This system, while still exploitative, provided some avenues for social mobility.

Slaves were used in the temple. Just penning the words makes me realize I am not sure I have ever asked the question, why? Why would a religious institution participate in the practice of slavery? I recognize that there are rules and regulations in the Old Testament for this practice. And yet there is something within my mind and heart that wants to question the justification. Although I can certainly understand slavery's function in the first-century economy, there is something within me that says that does not make it right or even good. I also recognize the thread tied to many religious leaders that endorsed slavery and referenced these practices in Scripture as justification. Perhaps I am judging yesterday's practices with today's moral standards, which is not always helpful or productive. Could it be that these practices of employing slaves in the temple system kept young women from exploitation? I could only hope.

The slave girl in Mark's Gospel has seemingly no power, no privilege, no right to speak up or out to Peter. And it is not lost on me that while Jesus stood before one of the most powerful men in Jerusalem, the high priest, he remained nearly silent. In the courtyard Peter was face-to-face with a slave girl and Peter could not stop talking. There's a clear juxtaposition here between the high priest and Jesus and the servant girl and Peter. And yet sometimes as a reader on this side of history we are quick to make Peter the focus. Poor Peter, at least he was in the temple courtyard. It's on the outer edges, but at least Peter was present, unlike the other eleven disciples.

It makes me wonder who does this slave girl think she is? Does she not understand her place in the temple system? Why was she speaking with so much courage and, dare I say, boldness to Peter? Could it be that the servant girl is not wanting to get Peter in trouble, but rather attempting to push him into action? Imagine with me for a moment that this young woman was trying to get Peter to actively come to Jesus's aid. Perhaps this servant girl experienced the words of Jesus during one of his many trips to Jerusalem. Did she stand on the temple steps when Jesus turned over the money changers' tables? Had she witnessed Jesus commending the widow for her offering? What if this girl was a witness to one of Jesus's many healings and miracles? If I dig even deeper into my imagination, what if her experience in the temple system was less than good? Some people, never sold into slavery, have experienced church hurt and exploitation at the hands of religious leaders. It's not difficult for me to imagine this woman's life being challenging, even horrific. While reading through the Passion narratives, I have been quick to assume the servant girl was just going right along with the crowd, hoping Peter would face the same fate as Jesus. But what if she was a gift of grace in Peter's life? What if she wanted Peter to fight for her and her people: "Peter, stand up. Peter, wake up. You were made for such a time as this!"

Certainly, throughout Mark's Gospel Jesus never displays a negative view of slaves. In fact, Jesus identified himself with them.

So Jesus called them and said to them, "You know that among the gentiles those whom they recognize as their rulers lord it over them, and their great ones are tyrants over them. But it is not so among you; instead, whoever wishes to become great among you must be your servant, and whoever wishes to be first among you must be slave of all. For the Son of Man came not to be served but to serve and to give his life a ransom for many."

Mark 10:42-45

Matthew identified Jesus as the suffering servant from Isaiah 53, "This was to fulfill what had been spoken through the prophet Isaiah, 'He took our infirmities and bore our diseases'" (Matthew 8:17). And the apostle Paul when writing to the church at Philippi quoted what was thought to be a common hymn or creed,

Let the same mind be in you that was in Christ Jesus, who, though he existed in the form of God, did not regard equality with God as something to be grasped, but emptied himself, taking the form of a slave, assuming human likeness.

Philippians 2:5-7

Jesus did not merely identify with servants, but seemingly routinely championed women as well. In Mark's Gospel Jesus healed the woman suffering from twelve years of bleeding on his way to raising Jairus's lifeless daughter from death (Mark 5:21-43). As we explored in chapter 1, Jesus championed the woman who anointed his feet and declared that we'd be talking about her for a long time. And here we discover this young, female slave courageously and boldly confronting one of Jesus's closest disciples.

Could it be that in Peter this servant woman did not see a criminal but rather a flicker of hope? She was on the bottom of the socioeconomic ladder looking for someone, anyone who could step up to change the circumstances of her life and those of her people. Just imagine with me that she had been sold into slavery because her family could not keep up with taxes required by Jerusalem and Rome. The servant girl's very freedom was bound by a system that kept the poor poorer and the rich and ruling class ever-gaining power and economic superiority. Perhaps she, too, had hoped that Jesus would be the one to right the wrongs and restore stability to a system of oppression.

Perhaps the servant girl's attempts to press Peter throughout the courtyard of Caiaphas's house was actually her begging him to take a risk. She wanted Peter to stand up to the powers that be and to advocate for Jesus and his release. If we read this scripture regarding her daily circumstance, perhaps she was a positive force in Peter's story. But why do you and I struggle to read the story that way? Perhaps it is because we reject the idea that opposition could ever be a force for good in our own stories as well.

Unlikely Opposition

Opposition usually does not feel great. Sometimes it's our human tendency to want life to be smooth, decisions easy, and our trajectory up and to the right. Certainly, I do not pretend to understand the life that the servant girl or even Peter faced in the first century. But I do recognize that facing opposition is not easy, and between the late-night prayer session with Jesus, the grief of Jesus's own words, and now Jesus's arrest that Peter does not have the mental, emotional, or physical capacity to resist.

Then after a little while the bystanders again said to Peter, "Certainly you are one of them, for you are a Galilean, and you talk like one." But he began to curse, and he swore an oath, "I

do not know this man you are talking about." At that moment
the cock crowed for the second time. Then Peter remembered
that Jesus had said to him, "Before the cock crows twice, you will
deny me three times." And he broke down and wept.

Mark 14:70b-72

Peter's accent gave him away. I cannot help hearing in my own native tongue, "You aren't from around here, are you?" Peter's "speak-first and think-later" practice did not serve him well in this moment. Peter denied Jesus first privately, then publicly, and then explicitly. It was a classic demonstration of apostasy.[4] His denial was a big deal. And although I really want Peter to get it, to wake up after the first denial, he does not. Peter did not get it. I mean the rooster did crow but it's interesting that Mark was the only Gospel writer who wrote that the rooster crowed twice. In the Gospels of Matthew, Luke, and John the rooster only crows one time, but here Peter gets a second chance to hear the alarm. Why didn't Peter wake up between the servant girl's question and the first call of the rooster? It takes that second rooster crow to ultimately open Peter's ears and eyes.

Jesus had warned him, "Truly I tell you, this day, this very night, before the cock crows twice, you will deny me three times" (Mark 14:30). But Peter wasn't convinced, "But he said vehemently, 'Even though I must die with you, I will not deny you.' And all of them said the same" (Mark 14:31). Peter was the ride-or-die disciple, the one who stepped out of boats, swung swords, and promised he would never abandon his cherished friend. And yet, here he was, standing by the fire, warming himself in the courtyard while Jesus faced death: First question. Denial. First crow. Second question. More denial. A third accusation. And then the rooster crowed a second time, and Peter was broken and distraught by his own denial. In that moment Peter realized he had done exactly what Jesus said he would. The sound of the rooster cut through his self-assurance and woke him up to a painful truth that he had failed the one he swore he would stand by.

But let's be honest: Peter is not the only one caught in moments of self-preservation. We all have our own inconvenient roosters. The voices, the moments, the reminders that shake us awake to what's right in front of us. Maybe it's a friend calling us out when we slip into comfort over conviction. Maybe it's someone on social media challenging us: are you really following Jesus or just admiring him from a distance? Maybe it's that moment when we scroll past yet another story of injustice, yet another hurting person, and something inside us says, "Do something, stand up, wake up!" These inconvenient roosters do not let us off the hook. They do not let us pretend we did not hear. They crow loud and clear, not to shame us, but to call us back to who we're meant to be, followers of Jesus.

And yet here's the good news: denial is not final. There is forgiveness. There is redemption. There is restoration. Peter's story did not end with his failure. Jesus doesn't leave him weeping in the courtyard. It's the moment when the young man dressed in a white robe singles out Peter for Jesus's direction post-Resurrection, "But go, tell his disciples and Peter that he is going ahead of you to Galilee; there you will see him, just as he told you" (Mark 16:7). After the Resurrection, Jesus meets him by another fire, not for retribution or rebuke but for the purpose of restoring Peter.

> When they had finished breakfast, Jesus said to Simon Peter, "Simon son of John, do you love me more than these?" He said to him, "Yes, Lord; you know that I love you." Jesus said to him,

"Feed my lambs." A second time he said to him, "Simon son of John, do you love me?" He said to him, "Yes, Lord; you know that I love you." Jesus said to him, "Tend my sheep." He said to him the third time, "Simon son of John, do you love me?" Peter felt hurt because he said to him the third time, "Do you love me?" And he said to him, "Lord, you know everything; you know that I love you." Jesus said to him, "Feed my sheep."

John 21:15-17

With "feed my sheep," Jesus once again invited Peter into the circle of belonging. And that's the hope you and I hold on to today. The roosters in our lives expose where we've fallen short, but they don't get the final crow. We received a second chance or maybe even a thirty-seventh chance. We are invited into something greater. The servant girl knew. Deep down Peter knew. And through her example, we discover the force of love that calls us, forgives us and calls us again. The question is, Will we wake up? Will we listen? Or will we keep pretending we do not hear? Because Jesus is always ready to restore, but first, we must face the truth about ourselves.

Back to hiking at Old Man's Cave and Cedar Falls. As I was arguing with everyone and no one or should I say as I was arguing mostly with God, I began to say, "But God, what about the people who are mean? But God, what if these people are wrong? But God, what if they do not love you or anyone back?" I was really determined to prove God wrong. And like the blanket of snow around me, God's love, revealed in Christ, is this ever-expanding mystery. God's love always creates a carpet of compassion and messes with my heart and mind. Suddenly I felt the urge to look around me to witness once again the glistening snow, the awe and wonder of God's good creation.

In that moment I was overwhelmed by awe, of the snow-covered trails, the towering cliffs, and the sheer depth, height, length, and breadth of God's scandalous love. It made me wonder: Why would I ever hoard God's love for myself? Why wouldn't I shower my neighbor, even my impossible or enemy neighbor, with that same glorious love? Who knew Father Gregory Boyle would play the role of a servant girl and get in my face, or rather I should say, stay in my ear, and challenge me to be who I say I am. I am a follower of Jesus, who believes and lives the tangible reality that everyone belongs to God, and we belong to one another. Certainly, an unlikely opposition, indeed.

Practice: Naming Your Unlikely Opposition

Opposition often comes from the least-expected places, and sometimes, the people who frustrate us the most are the ones teaching us something valuable. Maybe it's a coworker who constantly questions your decisions, a family member who never seems to understand you, or even a friend who challenges your beliefs. It's easy to dismiss these people as obstacles to our peace, but what if, instead, they are reflections of something deeper within us? What if God is using these moments of tension to refine us, to make us more patient, more self-aware, and more open to growth? Rather than resisting these interactions outright, we can begin to ask what they reveal about ourselves—our triggers, our pride, and perhaps even our own blind spots.

Consider the possibility that unlikely opposition can be a tool for spiritual awakening. Just as Jesus often faced resistance from the religious leaders of his time, we, too, may encounter pushback in our lives that serves a greater purpose. The person who irritates you may be holding up a mirror, revealing something God wants to work on in your heart and mind. Maybe their persistence is exposing an area of your life where you need more grace. Instead of seeing opposition as an enemy, could it be that God is using them as an instrument to wake you up to God's presence in unexpected ways? What if, instead of frustration, you leaned into curiosity, asking God, "What are you trying to show me through this person?"

Take a moment now to reflect and write it down. Who in your life is pushing your buttons? Whom do you wish would just stop challenging you? Instead of avoiding or resenting those people, what would happen if you approached the situation with a posture of humility and grace? Perhaps their opposition is not just an obstacle but an opportunity for transformation. Maybe, just maybe, what feels like resistance today will become a moment of grace tomorrow. Let's take a moment to pray and ask God to open our eyes to the deeper work God is doing through the people we least expect.

God of inconvenient roosters, thank you for speaking through unlikely people and uncomfortable moments. Open our hearts to receive your truth, even when it challenges us. Give us the courage to face our own denials and the grace to be restored by your love. Remind us daily that everyone belongs to you and to one another. Amen.

Chapter 3
UNLIKELY FREEDOM
Barabbas

The governor again said to them, "Which of the two do you want me to release for you?" And they said, "Barabbas."

Matthew 27:21

I find it natural to get caught up in the dichotomy of right and wrong. Perhaps it's because in childhood we are raised to believe that there are good guys and gals and bad guys and gals with no murky middle in-between. I revel in a good story that defines actors and their motives in the simplest forms. Even with my own children, I have a deep desire to help them understand that good always triumphs and those who engage in dubious practices face dire consequences. Barabbas was clearly a bad guy, a morally suspect character in the unfolding of God's story, or was he? Could it be that our freedom from shame is tied up in our understanding of people like Barabbas? I realize that in Barabbas I see a glimpse of myself and my deep desire to fight for what is right. Perhaps that's because I too want to avoid the pain of shame at all costs.

Shame, Shame

I sat on the living room floor combing through the pages of our family Bible. My momma kept this beautiful heirloom Bible on the bottom shelf of the entertainment center in our living room. Even as a young child, I had been taught how to clean and dust those shelves. Long before the days of the Swiffer dust mop and disposable rags, my mom always ensured that we filled a bucket with warm water and measured out the Murphy's Oil Soap. Too much Murphy's Oil and your hands would smell like the soap for days. The chore required yours truly to subsequently wash and then dry every single figurine, each knickknack, and every picture frame that occupied those shelves. The shelves were packed to overflowing with my mom's favorite items. Angels were tucked in-between photos of extended family members. Crosses and plaques were etched with scriptures and motivational memes. Each had its own hand-knit doily to ensure it never scratched the wood underneath. Although I did not love dusting, I did not loathe it either. There was something about completing the job and seeing all the dust removed that was terribly satisfying.

The Bibles were on the bottom self. "Be careful," my mom would always say. I was cautioned not to use too much water or even open the pages for fear of damaging the Bible. But I was so curious. I was determined to take a peek. The Bible was black;

its pages lined with gold on the outer edges. It was so thick and heavy that I struggled to pick it up. My little fingers fumbled to keep from dropping the Bible from its shelf. I had to lay it flat on the carpet to open it up. As I began opening the pages, it revealed places to keep a record of our family tree. I hovered over names that I could not quite read but was sure I recognized. I began to imagine what their lives were like. Did they too live on a farm? Did their children have to dust off shelves? What if I was doing the same chores that they had to complete? Daydreaming took me to a time when indoor plumbing was not a guarantee, and lights were a luxury many could not afford. And that's when it happened. Diverted by my imagination, I accidently turned the pages too quickly and tore a page in one of my mom's prized possessions.

"Oh no!" I said right out loud. I quickly closed the Bible and hid the torn page somewhere within the New Testament of the same Bible. My little heart raced as I heard my mother's voice. I could not let her find out that I had torn a page. She came around the corner with a bit of a frown on her face. "Rachel," she asked, "is everything okay?" I immediately lied and said, "Yes, Mom, everything is fine," and quickly whined about how long it took to dust the entire entertainment center. It must have been the tone of my voice that gave it away because she knew something was up. Moms always seem to know when their children are not sharing the full truth. She saw the Bible on the floor and opened it up to realize I had torn one of the pages. My mother was not happy with me! "I told you to be careful, Rachel!" she said with exasperation in her voice. It was not intentional, but her outward display of disappointment cut me to the core. "I can't believe you did this!" she clapped back. The tears began to pool in my eyes, my shoulders began to shake, and before I could say much of anything, my heart and head were full of shame.

I felt shame because I tore the page. I felt shame because I lied. I felt shame because I disappointed my momma. Shame is a like a weighted blanket. When it wraps itself around you, you can still move but you always feel its pressure crushing down on you. And I believe I am not alone in this experience of shame. Shame blankets our life experiences. Sometimes it feels like it is embedded in our human DNA. Shame is everywhere. Most people carry shame around as a constant companion. And it's no wonder. Shame begins with our family of origin. We hear stories in our families of family members who have made bad choices, many of them more intense than tearing the pages of the family Bible. It's the family member who landed themselves in jail. Other folks who were caught up in some form of addiction. Perhaps there was a brutal divorce in your family history.

Many people have long-kept secrets: a history of abuse, poverty, bankruptcy, or simply the awareness of not measuring up. Perhaps you grew up in a family where shame was the currency of the day. You did not meet expectations, spoken or unspoken. Because of your choices or the lack thereof you were labeled: the weird one, the outsider, the misfit, the black sheep, or even "the one who is not like the rest of us." I was talking to a friend the other day about the shame in her family and she recalled that even though all the siblings in her family received punishment for their lack of measuring up, it was the youngest sister who received a double portion of the shame. And no matter how hard the youngest tried, punishment seemed like her destiny. As adults they now realize that their parents, too, were operating out of shame. But their parents often were not aware of the shame they were carrying or the way shame manifested itself in their lives. Reader, I imagine the same could be true for you and me. When we are triggered, when we lash out, when we act in less than routine ways, shame is usually the source. Shame is what I call the thing behind the thing.

Shame is in those moments when our response to a coworker goes sideways. Shame rears its ugly head when frustration bubbles over and we yell at a child for making a simple mistake. We experience shame when our spouse calls us out on not completing a task that they asked us to do. We take shame to the internet, engaging in debates to prove who's right and who's wrong, as if certainty could quiet the discomfort inside us. Sometimes, we go to the opposite extreme, trying to shield our kids from the very missteps we once made, wrapping them in a protective bubble to spare them from the pain of failure. We work overtime to ensure no missteps are made at work, at home, or even within the church. We cling to control, we micromanage those around us, we decide every decision must be run by our desk. Whether through anger, control, or avoidance, these reactions reveal the subtle and not-so-subtle ways shame manifests in our daily lives.

Shame influences us in ways we do not always recognize. It can make us avoid difficult conversations, hold back affection, or internalize criticism, whether it's about what we have done or what we have left undone. Even now, I feel the sting of shame when someone points out a flaw or a missed opportunity. Several years ago, I had a message from a congregant that they wanted to meet with me to discuss a church matter. Immediately I assumed the worst. Of course I did. I, like many of my colleagues, had navigated COVID policies and procedures, racial tensions, political divides, LGBTQ+ inclusion, and regular criticism in church life. I assumed the conversation was going to be difficult because in that season almost every conversation was a difficult conversation. I braced myself, and then the person sat in my office to share just how much I had shaped their faith journey. The conversation was good! And I had to reflect on why I assumed that this person was carrying with them pain that they would later inflict on me. I knew in that moment I had some soul-searching to do. I, too, needed to get to the thing behind the thing. I had to tell myself the truth about my own shame. And I know I am not alone. At its core, shame is a universal human experience, shaping our interactions, our fears, and even our silence.

Shame showed up early in Genesis with Adam and Eve. God told them they could eat of all the fruits in God's created garden except for one. And surprise, surprise, they went for the fruit that was off-limits. God showed up early in the morning for their regular chat, but they were hiding because they felt, you guessed it, shame. Many people talk about original sin, but I think it's more helpful to talk about original shame. Guilt is not shame. Guilt can be a good force in our lives. Guilt says I made a bad choice. But shame is different. Sometimes in our shame we each tell ourselves "I am bad." And what happens when Adam, Eve, you, and I come face-to-face with our shame? We tend to blame. Shame leads to blame because we need a scapegoat!

We Need a Scapegoat

Turn on the news, scroll your social media feed, and you will discover our deep need to have someone to blame for the pain we experience as human beings. This is an old story. This is an origin story, and this is also Jesus's story. In the Gospel of Matthew 27,

Jesus had been captured by religious officials and had then been handed over to the Roman governor of Judea, Pontius Pilate. The Romans occupied this territory. Although the Jews had a degree of religious freedom and acceptance, they were expected to comply with the orders and, at times, the whims of Rome. And although the religious officials could have had Jesus stoned if they had chosen to do so, crucifixion was more commonly practiced by the Roman Empire. Crucifixion was beyond the scope of the Sanhedrin. Pilate did not seem to know exactly what to do with Jesus of Nazareth, but Pilate could read the room and was cued in to the fact that this crowd needed someone to blame:

> Now at the festival the governor was accustomed to release a prisoner for the crowd, anyone whom they wanted. At that time they had a notorious prisoner called Jesus Barabbas. So after they had gathered, Pilate said to them, "Whom do you want me to release for you, Jesus Barabbas or Jesus who is called the Messiah?" For he realized that it was out of jealousy that they had handed him over.
>
> Matthew 27:15-18

Life for regular folk in first-century Judea was not exactly easy. The rich were getting richer, and the poor were barely hanging on by their fingernails. Many would-be rebels had revolted against the likes of Rome. The memory of the Maccabean Revolt lingered in the minds of first-century Jews, shaping their hopes and frustrations under Roman rule. This revolt, which took place in the second century BCE, was a defining moment in Jewish history. Led by Judas Maccabeus and his brothers, the Jewish rebels successfully overthrew the Greek Seleucid rulers, reclaiming and rededicating the desecrated temple in Jerusalem. Their victory, celebrated annually during Hanukkah, was more than just a military triumph, it was a testament to God's faithfulness and the possibility of liberation from foreign oppressors.[1] For generations, this story inspired the Jewish people, serving as a powerful reminder that even against overwhelming odds, deliverance was indeed possible.

However, by the time of Jesus, the power of Rome cast a far darker shadow over Jewish aspirations. The might of the Roman Empire, embodied by figures like Pontius Pilate, made the idea of an armed rebellion seem like little more than a pipe dream. Unlike the Greeks, whose rule had been successfully resisted, Rome's dominance was absolute and enforced with brutal efficiency. The people longed for another Judas Maccabeus, a leader who could drive out their oppressors and restore their people's freedom. Rome was quick to keep Pax Romana, Peace of Rome, and regularly used lethal force to do so. Many factions of thought emerged when attempting to understand just how to navigate Jewish identity in Caesar's territories.

Perhaps you can see yourself or even your own political persuasions in these first-century Jewish sects. Each sect had its own strategy for survival under the iron grip of Rome. The Pharisees were the teachers, the interpreters of the Law. They were the Jews who believed that holiness was not just for the temple but for everyday life. Their resistance was not through swords but through meticulous obedience to Torah. These faithful adherents to the law distinguished themselves apart in devotion, hoping that if enough people practiced faithfully, maybe, just maybe, God would move. It is important to note that when reading through the New Testament, the Pharisees emerge as Jesus's biggest adversaries.

Sadducees were priests and although some were elites and temple power brokers, many lived away from Jerusalem. It was only those at the top, for example the chief priest, and small priestly family that held the power. They were the ones who cozied up to Rome just enough to keep the status quo.[2] They controlled the priesthood, maintained the sacrifices, and made sure that their way of life was not disturbed. They also did not believe in resurrection, and belief in resurrection was popular among the people. It's unclear as to why the Sadducees faded from history. Perhaps if they were the aristocracy of the faith, they were wiped out by Rome in the Jewish revolt.

Then there are the Essenes. Although never directly mentioned in the New Testament, John the Baptist was thought to be an Essene. These folks lived out in the desert. Their lifestyle was very similar to desert Fathers and Mothers of the Christian faith. The Essenes seemed to pack up, leave the city, and hunker down in the desert. They believed that if they would merely keep themselves pure and set apart, God would come and set everything right.[3] They, too, were serious about scholarship and preserving writings. In the Qumran region, tucked into desert caves, the Dead Sea Scrolls were discovered. Scholars believe these scrolls to be the work of a marginal small group of Essenes.[4] The Essenes were waiting, writing, fasting, praying, and preparing for a divine intervention.

And then there were the Zealots. The Roman Empire did not particularly appreciate the Zealots. There was mention of the Zealots in the New Testament. For example, Simon the Zealot was cited as one of Jesus's twelve disciples:

These are the names of the twelve apostles: first, Simon (who is called Peter) and his brother Andrew; James son of Zebedee,

*and his brother John; Philip and Bartholomew; Thomas
and Matthew the tax collector; James son of Alphaeus,
and Thaddaeus; Simon the Zealot and Judas Iscariot, who
betrayed him.*

Matthew 10:2-4 NIV

In their work, *The New Testament in Its World*, N. T. Wright
and Michael Bird questioned distinguishing Zealots as a separate
Jewish sect, "Many scholars have long assumed some kind of
'zealot' party that existed in the first century, to which Jesus's
follower 'Simon the Zealot' purportedly belonged. It appears
more likely, however, that there were, throughout the first century,
many movements which laid claim to the tradition of active 'zeal,'
a tradition that went back, through the Maccabees, to the cultural
memory of Phinehas and Elijah."[5] No matter the case, Zealots
refused to bow, refused to compromise, and believed the only way
to freedom was through revolution. Possessing daggers in their
cloaks and fire in their bellies, the Zealots were ready to spill
Roman blood to hasten the coming kingdom of God.

And Jesus of Nazareth was appealing to those with zeal,
saying things like:

> *"Do not think that I have come to bring peace to the earth; I
> have not come to bring peace but a sword. For I have come to
> set a man against his father, and a daughter against her mother,
> and a daughter-in-law against her mother-in-law, and one's
> foes will be members of one's own household."*
>
> *Matthew 10:34-36*

Jesus sounded like a rebel! So it was no wonder Zealots were
attracted to Jesus. And yet when the religious leaders came to

arrest Jesus, he was clear: put away your sword. Wait a minute Jesus. Aren't you going to fight for what is right? Even the Zealots needed a scapegoat. They, too, wanted someone to blame.

Matthew sets up the scenario known as the Paschal Pardon or the pardon at Passover. There is no documented example of this in Old Testament or even in other Jewish literature of a Paschal Pardon. Seemingly these kinds of pardons are a Roman practice or possibly more ancient than that penned in Babylonian lore.[6] And Matthew pointed to the choice at hand: "So after they had gathered, Pilate said to them, 'Whom do you want me to release for you, Jesus Barabbas or Jesus who is called the Messiah?'" (Matthew 27:17).

A choice between two Jesuses: Jesus the Messiah or Jesus Barabbas. Jesus Barabbas is the man we know so little about, yet his name echoes through the Passion story like a haunting refrain. The Gospel writers tell us he was a notorious prisoner, "at that time they had a notorious prisoner called Jesus Barabbas" (Matthew 27:16). Or Barabbas was an insurrectionist: "Now a man called Barabbas was in prison with the insurrectionists who had committed murder during the insurrection" (Mark 15:7). He was labeled a murderer in the Gospel of Luke: "(This was a man who had been put in prison for an insurrection that had taken place in the city and for murder)" (23:19). It's clear Barabbas was a rebel against Rome. But was he more than just a common criminal? Some scholars speculate he was a Zealot. If that's true, then the choice Pilate offered was not just between two men. The choice was between two visions of salvation. Barabbas embodied the fight-for-your-life, take-up-arms, let's-kill-our-way-to-freedom mindset that some believed was the only way out from under Caesar's thumb. Can you imagine what Barabbas was thinking? Perhaps he wanted to be there, detained by the likes of Rome. Inspired by the crowd, he was not asking for a pardon. No way! Barabbas knew what he had signed up for, he wanted to die a martyr's death. Barabbas was fighting for the very people he sought to protect from Rome. If I could get in Barabbas's head, perhaps I would find that there was pride for what he had done. Maybe he thought to himself, I fought my way to be here. I know why I am standing before the people, but what about this Jesus of Nazareth? What did this guy do to tick off this crowd?

What if Barabbas was tired of occupation? What if he was weary of oppression, of living under the crushing weight of a foreign empire dictating his every move? Could it be that Barabbas was not merely a criminal but a man desperate for agency over his own life, someone who saw no other way but violence to reclaim what had been stripped from him? In his eyes, perhaps, he was not a rebel but a freedom fighter, driven by a conviction that resistance, even through force, was the only path to justice. His actions led him to prison, facing the inevitable consequences of his choices, and yet, at the last moment, he was spared. But what if, in that moment of release, he was forced to confront an even deeper battle within himself?

What if Barabbas, standing in the presence of Jesus, felt a shame he had never expected? What if, rather than dying for what he had fought for, he was left to wrestle with the reality that someone else was taking his place? Did he wonder whether his cause had been in vain? Did he feel resentment that he had been freed while Jesus, a man who preached peace rather than violence, was condemned? Could it be that, like so many others, he turned on Jesus, seeking someone to blame for his inner turmoil? I am not justifying Barabbas's crime, but rather, I am naming the undeniable truth that many are willing to fight, even to the point of death, for what they believe is right, especially when they are fueled by anger, fear, or both. What if now Barabbas has to live with the grief that he failed his cause and, in his shame, he wanted someone to blame.

We are always looking for someone to blame, a place to unload the twisted feelings we experience when tragedy or hardship strikes. When a mass shooting occurs, the media and the public quickly speculate, debating whether the problem lies in mental health, gun laws, or societal decay. Instead of pausing to grieve or understand, many rush to assign fault, hoping that if they can name the cause, they can regain a sense of control. The same thing happens when a plane crashes. Immediate blame is cast on pilots, faulty aircraft design, or even meteorologists who failed to predict hazardous weather. Rather than acknowledging the complexity of such events, our culture demands a scapegoat, someone to bear responsibility for our fear and helplessness.

This impulse to assign blame is deeply ingrained in our human nature and extends far beyond major national tragedies. When the economy struggles, we blame politicians, immigrants, or large corporations for taking away jobs. If a sports team loses a crucial game, fans blame the coach, the referees, or even a single player who made a mistake. As a major fan of The Ohio State Buckeyes, I know this reality all too well. After the OSU football team lost to the Michigan Wolverines for the fourth year in a row, many took to verbal violence against head coach Ryan Day and his family. Rumors swirled that even teachers accosted his children in their classrooms. Day was forced to hire extra security for his family home because the threat was so intense. Humans need someone to blame!

When our teams are losing, our livelihood is threatened, our family is in danger, or our reputation is on the line, we instinctively look for someone to accuse. It's easier to point fingers than to sit with discomfort, uncertainty, or the possibility that some problems have no easy solution. Blame gives us a false sense of resolution, but it rarely leads to healing or real change. Back in God's garden in Genesis, God has called Adam and Eve out for hiding. God wanted to stay in relationship with Adam and Eve. But in their shame, Adam and Eve were quick to blame:

> *The man said, "The woman whom you gave to be with me, she gave me fruit from the tree, and I ate." Then the* LORD *God said to the woman, "What is this that you have done?" The woman said, "The serpent tricked me, and I ate."*
>
> Genesis 3:12-13

The exchange between Adam, Eve, and God could seem comical, if it did not ring true of our human experience. Blame seems like the best way out. We need a scapegoat. But then in a strange twist of events, Jesus flips the script, taking the shame and blame onto himself.

Willing Scapegoat

The writer of the Gospel of Matthew was making a point loud and clear. Matthew was setting up this whole moment like a Jewish purification ritual, and the symbolism is thick. Pilate washing his hands was not just some passive gesture. His handwashing mirrored what the priests did before offering a sacrifice. Imagine with me the priest in the temple, preparing to make the sacrifice. Before he approaches the altar, he undergoes a meticulous process of purification, washing his hands and feet at the bronze basin to ensure he is ritually clean. He then put on his sacred vestments, garments set apart for this holy duty. Each piece symbolized his role as a mediator between God and the people. With earnestness, he lays his hands upon the animal, symbolically transferring the sins of the people onto the sacrifice, a profound moment of intercession; the animal taking on the sins of the people. What if, with this one gesture, the Gospel writer was preparing us for what's coming next? Jesus becoming the willing scapegoat, Jesus a symbol of the sacrifice made on the Day of Atonement. Even the crowd and their response to Pilate reminds me of the symbolism of sacrifice: "His blood be on us and on our children!" (Matthew 27:25). At first, I find their response strange or even cruel. But after further consideration, I realize the Gospel writer could be inviting the reader to dig deeper into the meaning of atonement.

During the Day of Atonement, the high priest would wash his hands prior to sprinkling blood on the lid of the atonement seat also known as the mercy seat. First to cover Israel's ritual impurities, but also their moral failings.[7] It's believed that God's presence touched earth on that very seat and that God provided the substitute. But the ritual did not stop with the sprinkling of blood in holy spaces. A second goat was used and this time the sins of Israel were placed on its head and then it was sent into the wilderness:

> Then Aaron shall lay both his hands on the head of the live goat and confess over it all the iniquities of the Israelites, and all their transgressions, all their sins, putting them on the head of the goat and sending it away into the wilderness by means of someone designated for the task. The goat shall bear on itself all

> *their iniquities to a barren region, and the goat shall be set free*
> *in the wilderness.*
>
> *Leviticus 16:21-22*

Perhaps the Gospel writer was connecting the dots between old and new sacrifices. Standing before the people are two Jesuses, two potential scapegoats. And Jesus of Nazareth, the ultimate scapegoat, did not resist, did not fight back, but was willing to take on the weight of sin, rejection, and shame. More than a mere ritual of purification, Pilate's washing of his hands led to substitution:

> *The governor again said to them, "Which of the two do you*
> *want me to release for you?" And they said, "Barabbas." Pilate*
> *said to them, "Then what should I do with Jesus who is called*
> *the Messiah?" All of them said, "Let him be crucified!" Then he*
> *asked, "Why, what evil has he done?" But they shouted all the*
> *more, "Let him be crucified!"*
>
> *Matthew 27:21-23*

Matthew wanted us to see Jesus standing in for all of us. Barabbas went free, the crowd carried on, Pilate tried to wash off the guilt, but Jesus? He took it all. Substitutionary atonement is a part of Christian theology, this belief that Jesus did not just die, he died for us and instead of us. But let me be honest, this entire moment of the crowd choosing Barabbas over Jesus feels a little too neat and theologically loaded. Some scholars even wonder if this was a later addition to the Passion story, designed to reinforce the idea that Jesus was not just another crucified revolutionary, but the one sent to take our place. I wrestle with the theology of substitutionary atonement, not because I do not believe that atonement is important, but rather because Jesus's death seems bigger than a mere trade. Jesus's death seems more cosmic than just a one-for-one. Because what I know is that Jesus's life, death, and resurrection bring healing and restoration to all of God's broken creation. Barabbas's experience draws us back to the beginning, to that place of original shame, where humanity first wrestled with guilt, fear, and the desire to shift blame. His story lingers in the shadows of history, an unsettling reflection of our own struggle with freedom and responsibility. Was his release a moment of redemption or a haunting reminder of the weight of sin? In his place, Jesus was condemned. This trade feels both deliberate and mysterious, as if echoing something ancient, something woven into the fabric of our deepest longing for grace and forgiveness.

Too often when we read the story of Jesus Barabbas, we may want to tell Pilate, "You got the wrong guy!" Barabbas deserved to die. In our Easter pageants and church cantatas, we wince in response to the crowd's "Crucify him, crucify him," because we want to believe there was no way we would have ever gotten caught up in the frenzy, thereby ushering in Jesus's death. Honestly, when I read through these Passion narratives, I, too, want to place blame, to separate the good guys and gals from the bad. I want to be on the winning team. I want to be on team Jesus.

By standing in the place of Barabbas, Jesus bears witness to the futility of violence, revealing that power built on force and bloodshed ultimately leads to emptiness. By becoming the scapegoat, Jesus makes space for the crowd to be their very human selves, full of fear, anger, and uncertainty, just as we are. In Jesus's sacrifice, he absorbs the weight of their judgment, their need for retribution, and in doing so, offers a different way forward. By taking on the role of the scapegoat, Jesus frees us from the endless cycle of blame and from the impulse to point fingers or pick sides to justify ourselves. His presence in that moment invites us into something deeper. Jesus invites us into an invitation to grace, to release, to a kind of justice that is not about retribution but about transformation.

In the musical *Dear Evan Hansen*, Evan makes a big mistake. He leads everyone to believe that he's besties with the kid who's been bullying him. It's the story of how a little white lie snowballs into a massive deception: bullying, dishonesty, shame, and the destructive nature of social media are all in there. But what ultimately sets Evan free is sharing his truth about a friend he never had and the pain of loneliness he experienced. It's his truth that sets Evan free. In her book *Daring Greatly*, Brené Brown identified the Shame 1-2-3s, reminding, "We all have it....We're all afraid to talk about shame. The less we talk about shame, the more control it has over our lives."[8]

I understand many of us have been trained in the art of keeping shame to ourselves. We do not talk about shame. When we keep shame to ourselves, we run the risk of operating out of anger, bitterness, or violence. Shame and blame are carried around like old, heavy blankets, as we drag them from one season of life to the next. We, like Barabbas, believe the only way to win is to fight, but there is a way out. What if instead, we lose the shame and blame?

Lose the Shame and Blame

Jesus never asked us to carry the weight of the world or the heaviness of our own personal shame for that matter. Jesus came to lift the burden, to free us from that weight, to heal us from the inside out. If I'm honest, there's still this little girl inside of me, the one who always wanted to get it right. A little girl who felt real shame when she didn't get it right and who still, every now and then, cringes at the thought of messing up. Sometimes, I have to stop and comfort her. I must remind her that she is loved, not for her perfection, not for her performance, but just because she is a beloved child of God. And maybe you need to do the same.

Jesus did not come just for the ones who had it all together. He did not look at Barabbas, the guilty one, the one set free in his place, and say, "I'll die for you, but I'll never forget what you did." Jesus took Barabbas's shame as well, absorbed his blame, and let him walk away free. And Jesus is doing the same for us. Whatever shame you're carrying, the guilt, the regret, the should-have-done-betters, give it to Jesus. Jesus is willing to take it and unlike many humans, Jesus will not use it against you. He will not hold your past blunders over your head. He will not remind you of it every time you try to move forward. Instead, Jesus whispers the truth that you are forgiven. You are loved. You are free.

So today, lay your shame down. Stop picking at the shame, stop replaying the failures, stop believing the lie that we or anyone else must earn grace. Jesus already took the shame, already made a way. And when the voice of shame tries to creep back in, speak louder. Speak truth. Remind yourself, and that little kid inside, that you are not defined by your worst moments. You are defined by the love of the One who refuses to hold anything against you. And that, my Reader is enough. Lose the shame and the blame, that is your unlikely freedom.

Practice: Letting Go of Shame

As we come to the close of this chapter, I want to invite you into a moment of reflection and release. In baptism, we are claimed as God's beloved. But too often, we carry around shame that was never ours to hold. Today, I want to remind you: you are claimed, not shamed. The weight of your past, the burden of guilt, the lies that whisper "not enough" do not have the final word. Jesus does. And Jesus's word is freedom.

Perhaps you will engage in a practice where you will write down the shame you are carrying. Perhaps in a small group or worship service you could pass out a small piece of dissolvable paper. Give people a moment to write down a word or phrase representing a shame they've carried. Maybe it's a mistake, a regret, or something spoken over you that made you believe you weren't worthy of love. Set up a baptism font or even clear bowls of water. Remind people baptismal waters are the same waters that claim them as God's beloved. Invite them forward to place their paper in the water to dissolve.

This is a sign and a symbol: shame does not get to define us anymore. Just as the paper disappears, so does the power of shame when we release it into God's grace.

Holy and loving God, we come before you carrying burdens you never asked us to bear. But today, in the waters of baptism, we remember the truth: we are claimed, not shamed. We release our shame into your grace. May we walk forward knowing we are loved, forgiven, and free. In the name of the One who took our place, Jesus Christ. Amen.

Chapter 4
UNLIKELY COMPANIONSHIP
Simon of Cyrene

As they led him away, they seized a man, Simon of Cyrene, who was coming from the country, and they laid the cross on him and made him carry it behind Jesus.

Luke 23:26

Sometimes life hands us an unlikely but steady companion. We did not ask for it, we did not go looking for it. This companion discovers us along life's journey. And much like Simon of Cyrene, we did not choose it; it chose us.

I imagine many of us have received that fateful phone call, the one we did not expect to receive. For me, the call and the space were very unusual. It is not every day that a venture capitalist maximizes a warehouse for creative new ventures, but Houston, Texas, was the exception. I was eagerly gathered with nearly one hundred church leaders and pastors with a collective passion for digital discipleship. These futurists deeply love Jesus and wonder how new digital methods could possibly connect real people to real people. And perhaps that real connection could ultimately lead people to faith in Jesus.

Although I am sure the presenters for the day were inspiring, I had to step out for an important phone call from my younger sister Julie. At first, I merely walked the concrete floors. Each step echoed against the adjacent walls, and the longer I walked the more intentional I became with where I was stepping. The space was massive. The construction was fresh and new, but the sheer volume of concrete communicated an industrial feel. The atmosphere was cool, but not warm. After passing people in office spaces, I attempted to find some semblance of quiet in the food court, but with no such luck. Desperate for privacy, I made my way up to the garden on the roof. The view was majestic, and in any other moment, I could have experienced the awe and wonder; but that day I simply needed a place to listen unseen. Julie had me on speaker phone as she, my parents, and I talked with an oncologist at the James Cancer Research Hospital. The James is in Columbus, one of the best in the state, and we knew it was my mom's best shot at effective treatment. Her oncologist explained in detail my mom's path forward. The call was not brief. The doctor was gentle and kind, but she did not sugarcoat the situation. "Pancreatic cancer does not have a high survival rate," she stated. Those words felt like a thousand pounds of concrete on my chest. We already knew that my mom's tumor was in a precarious position and the best shot of extending her life was to have something called a Whipple procedure to remove it. The surgery was not a guarantee the cancer would be eradicated, but it could potentially lengthen my mother's life. By now I was sitting in a small space that housed the building elevator, tucked away under the corner of the roof. And although I could hear a handful of people walking on and off the elevator, no one person could see or hear me, for which I was grateful. I kept my phone on mute most of the time, not wanting my parents to hear the elevator or my sobs as I learned more information concerning my mom's condition.

I Didn't Sign Up for This

Perhaps you've had a moment when you, too, found yourself in a place of desperation, tears streaming down your face, whispering to anyone and to no one, "I didn't sign up for this." Maybe it was in the sterile silence of a hospital room, the diagnosis settling over you like a fog, suffocating and unshakable. "I didn't sign up for this." Maybe your moment was in the bustle of your inbox, staring at an email from your boss that upended everything you thought was secure, we regret to inform you that..."I didn't sign up for this." Perhaps it was in the stunned stillness of your kitchen, hands wrapped around your coffee mug so tight you imagine you might crush it. The person you had pledged your forever to sighed deeply and said, "I just don't love you anymore." You do not know what to think or even what to say and yet bubbling in your mind is "I didn't sign up for this!" It's that feeling of dread when your young adult child calls from the police station sharing through tears that they are in trouble, and they need your help. As you grab your keys you exhale with "I didn't sign up for this." Or maybe it was under the blinding stadium lights, the weight of your coach's words knocking the breath from your lungs. "The doctor has said, 'your playing days are over.'" And in those moments, your knees hit the ground, the air feels too thick to breathe, and your heart aches with the sting of "this was never the plan." What do you do then?

You did not sign up for this! Life seems to hand us moments that we did not willingly agree to experience. Most days we just want to embrace the good, go with what is comfortable, and avoid the conflict; but sometimes life hands us situations that we simply cannot ignore. And in Luke's Gospel, that certainly rings true for Simon of Cyrene.

Cyrene is located in modern-day Shahhat, Libya, off the northern coast of the continent of Africa. The trip from Cyrene to Jerusalem is over 850 miles. Making that trip today would be like walking from Columbus, Ohio, to the Gulf of Mexico. Even if he traveled by ship, it would have taken him weeks to arrive in Jerusalem. According to the Book of Acts, there was a Jewish community in Cyrene and the group was present when Simon Peter preached his sermon on Pentecost. In a beautiful description of the diversity of pilgrims within Jerusalem for the feast of Pentecost the author described:

> *And at this sound the crowd gathered and was bewildered, because each one heard them speaking in the native language of each. Amazed and astonished, they asked, "Are not all these who are speaking Galileans? And how is it that we hear, each of us, in our own native language? Parthians, Medes, Elamites, and residents of Mesopotamia, Judea and Cappadocia, Pontus and Asia, Phrygia and Pamphylia, Egypt and the parts of Libya belonging to Cyrene, and visitors from Rome, both Jews and proselytes, Cretans and Arabs—in our own languages we hear them speaking about God's deeds of power."*
>
> *Acts 2:6-11*

Very little is known about Simon from Cyrene. Scripture did not describe Simon as a Jew, although one could assume he is in Jerusalem for the celebration of Passover. It is possible that this experience was Simon's first time traveling to Jerusalem. And if it is, could we together imagine his experience?

Filled with awe and wonder, the city was more vibrant and chaotic than he had ever imagined. Jerusalem's streets were packed with merchants calling out their wares. They were persistent, with desperation in their eyes, some nearly grabbing Simon by the arm on more than one occasion. The scent of roasted lamb and fresh bread filled the air. Simon's stomach began to rumble. His heart nearly pounding out of his chest. It was more chaotic and wonderful than he could have ever imagined. Simon moved carefully through the crowd, his travel-worn feet brushing against the dust of ancient roads. The temple, grand and awe-inspiring, loomed in the distance; its white stone reflecting the midday sun. Were those tears streaming down his face? He had been saving for a lifetime for this pilgrimage, and he was finally here. Jerusalem was the land he had longed to see, what he had journeyed so far to witness. And the temple was a holy place, a sacred space where heaven and earth touched.

As Simon made his way among throngs of pilgrims the noise shifted. Shouts rose from an unseen source. These voices were different. Instead of sounding desperate, they were thick with urgency and anger. Suddenly he noticed Roman soldiers pushing a man forward, his back bent under the weight of a wooden beam. Simon stepped forward to get a closer look. Blood stained the stranger's brow where a crude crown of thorns dug into his skin. Simon winced, but he could not look away. He watched, transfixed. The man stumbled, collapsing onto the street, his breath ragged. He did not mean to, but Simon cried out. And that was when the soldier noticed him. His response was a reflex; he could not help himself! Was it compassion or merely a plea for human decency? Before Simon could turn away, one of the soldiers grabbed him by the arm. Now he went from compassion to absolute terror! "Carry his cross!" The words were not a request but a command. Confused, Simon was trying to attempt to process what the soldier was saying. He was only a visitor, a mere tourist. Simon didn't sign up for this! He quickly looked away from the soldier and into the eyes of the suffering man. Who is this? There was something in those eyes, the pain, the exhaustion, and yet something deeper that felt like love that would not let him go. Simon lingered for a moment staring at this man's expression that nearly took his breath away. Simon's mind was racing. The questions just kept coming, Who is he? What did he do? Why is he being crucified? But there's no time for answers. The Roman soldiers have a job to do; they are angrily relentless and compel Simon to move forward. "Take the cross, now!"

And so, Simon did as he was told. He lifted the rugged wooden beam onto his shoulders. It was heavier than he expected. Its splinters pressed into his skin as he followed the condemned man through a nearly violent crowd. Step by step he walked with the man, a stranger bound to another's suffering. The walk was painful not merely because of the weight of the beam, but because he began to understand something very different was happening. This man was no mere religious rebel. Of course, many were condemning the man with their words but there were others who were following him. Many women, whose faces were struck deep with grief, reached out to touch this criminal. How could so much love and hate coexist in one place? The weight seemed unbearable, but something strange was happening. Although Simon's body ached, his heart and his head stirred. He did not know this man, but he felt that somehow this moment was more than just a forced burden, more than a mere command by a Roman soldier. He did not sign up for this and yet there was no mistake, this moment was an invitation, a calling into something greater.

With very little written about Simon of Cyrene, his full story is left to the imagination. He is only mentioned once in the Gospels of Matthew, Mark, and Luke, and not at all in John's Gospel. John did not mention Simon of Cyrene because the Jesus in John's Gospel did not need help to the cross. The author of the Gospel of John emphasizes the divinity of Jesus. Jesus seemed to be in control of the entire situation even on the cross. And although Matthew and Mark mention Simon, he seemed more willing than forced to carry the cross in those Gospels. Luke, however, described Simon as more of an innocent bystander, a visitor of the city of Jerusalem, minding his own business when he is pulled into the story:

> As they led him away, they seized a man, Simon of Cyrene, who was coming from the country, and they laid the cross on him and made him carry it behind Jesus. A great number of the people followed him, and among them were women who were beating their breasts and wailing for him.
>
> Luke 23:26-27

Can you imagine? You travel to Jerusalem for a holy festival, encountering a community party and unbeknownst to you, you get caught up in the mad dash of a funeral procession. Jewish rebels were being led outside the city gates. They were directed by the Romans to a high-visibility location where everyone could and would observe the Crucifixion. The Romans wanted it that way; crucifixion served as a human billboard to signal this is what happens to those who mess with Rome. I know humans are curious creatures but most of us avoid such displays of suffering. And in the modern Western world we have become obsessed with avoiding suffering at all costs, especially suffering that involves death. We shield ourselves from the hard, sanitize the pain for next generations, and work overtime to extend human life.

We live in a culture where people use potions and procedures to lengthen their lives, striving to push back aging, pain, and discomfort. From serums to surgery, from experimental gene therapies to extreme fasting regimens, the desire to outwit mortality is ever present. Technology entrepreneur Bryan Johnson exemplifies this pursuit. Johnson has dedicated millions of dollars and countless hours to reversing the effects of aging. His pursuit of the so-called foundation of youth is a full-time job. Johnson subjects himself to rigorous routines, medical interventions, and restrictive diets in the hope of extending his lifespan indefinitely. This man literally wants to live forever! Although Johnson's efforts may seem over-the-top, I recognize some of my own nighttime routines and exercise regimens are designed to maximize youthfulness and living as long as humanly possible. The desire to somehow defeat death and live forever is real. While advancements in medicine and wellness have improved the quality of life for many, there are many underlying questions, like why? Why are we so obsessed with avoiding suffering? Why attempt to conquer mortality? Is it simply human nature to resist pain, or does this relentless pursuit of longevity reveal something deeper? When I think about it long enough, I realize some are afraid of insignificance. Humans tend to want their lives to matter, their time on this terrestrial ball to count. Other people may fear the unknown. Is this all there is? There is quite the mystery concerning what may happen after this life. Even people of faith can have serious spiritual anxiety about what happens next and the realities of heaven.

Our resistance to suffering is not just about physical pain. Our resistance extends into our emotional and relational lives as well. Many people avoid hard conversations, choosing silence over the discomfort of addressing conflict. In workplaces, employees would rather quit than confront a toxic boss. In families, long-standing grudges fester because no one wants to risk the vulnerability required for reconciliation. Even in friendships, some people ghost each other instead of enduring an awkward but necessary difficult conversation. Social media has further enabled avoidance. People are enabled to hide behind anonymous screen names to avoid consequence and conflict. Some people curate versions of their lives where only the polished, happy moments are on display, shielding themselves from the messiness of real human connection. We crave ease and comfort, yet in doing so, we often sacrifice depth and authenticity.

The avoidance of suffering is also deeply ingrained in our habits of consumption and deep desire to be entertained. We turn to endless distractions: streaming services, video games, alcohol, or social media scrolling. These drugs of choice serve to numb emotional discomfort. Instead of sitting with grief or wrestling with difficult questions, we escape into virtual realities or medicate ourselves with retail therapy, comfort food, and self-help trends that promise quick fixes. I know I have had to tell myself the truth about myself on more than one occasion. I am quick to get caught up in social media videos and reels. Some videos can be extremely informative. But I start scrolling and before I know it, hours have passed. In what feels like the blink of an eye, I have lost track of time, and a big chunk of my day has vanished. Why do I do it? I want to numb my mind and heart and am determined to step out of the discomfort of my reality for a moment. We have created a culture where discomfort is not just something to be managed but something to be eradicated entirely. And yet in numbing our pain we also numb our capacity for growth. Sometimes we limit our opportunity for resilience. Could it be that by numbing the pain, we shut ourselves off to the unexplored dimensions of being alive?

Ironically, history and faith traditions tell us that suffering is often the very experience that refines us. I know I wore out my *A Night in Rocketown* CD in college. The song that always gave me pause was Ginny Owens's "If You Want Me To." At three years old Ginny became blind. As she was giving her testimony, she started to recite from James 1, "My brothers and sisters, whenever you face various trials, consider it all joy, because you know that the testing of your faith produces endurance. And let endurance complete its work, so that you may be complete and whole, lacking in nothing" (James 1:2-4). My young adult mind could not comprehend how suffering had anything to do with joy, let alone serve as experience for growth. The longer I've been alive, the more I recognize that great creativity is born from struggle.

Artists like Frida Kahlo are examples of humans whose work was deeply shaped by personal suffering. After a near-fatal bus accident at age eighteen, she endured chronic pain, multiple surgeries, and emotional turmoil. Kahlo's life was not easy, smooth, or comfortable, and yet she turned that pain into powerful self-portraits. Her art explores identity, resilience, and suffering. She does not ignore the pain, but rather authentically portrays just how beautifully horrific suffering can be. Paintings such as *The Two Fridas* (*Las dos Fridas*) vividly depict her physical and emotional wounds. Hearts outside their chests, these two women are bound together. One expression of Frida highlights her European heritage, while the other draws one to her deep Mexican roots. Frida does not avoid hard conversations. She creates portraits that serve as declarations of strength and survival. Instead of running from suffering, Kahlo embraced suffering as an intrinsic part of her art. She utilized her experience of pain and suffering to express something profoundly human.

These messages are found not merely in art and music. Wisdom is forged in hardship. Relationships can be deepened when they withstand trials. And yet sometimes we humans persist in fleeing anything unpleasant, seeking shortcuts to sanitize our existence. But what if we embraced suffering, rather than avoided it? Could suffering lead us to a fuller life? What if, like Simon of Cyrene, we could find meaning not in escaping burdens but in carrying them? Even when some circumstances are dropped upon us unexpectedly? The question is not whether we might avoid suffering; sometimes we will. Honestly, that, too, is part of being human. But could we allow suffering to shape our lives and experiences into something more beautiful? I have grown to experience suffering as mystery. I do not crave suffering in some kind of masochistic way, but I do not avoid it. There is something beautifully horrific about experiencing some forms of suffering. And perhaps that's because we do not suffer alone. Beauty is revealed in the gift of one another. There was a certain beauty expressed that day as Simon prevented Jesus from carrying the cross alone:

> As they led him away, they seized a man, Simon of Cyrene, who was coming from the country, and they laid the cross on him and made him carry it behind Jesus. A great number of the people followed him, and among them were women who were beating their breasts and wailing for him. But Jesus turned to them and said, "Daughters of Jerusalem, do not weep for me, but weep for yourselves and for your children. For the days are surely coming when they will say, 'Blessed are the barren, and the wombs that never bore, and the breasts that never nursed.' Then they will begin to say to the mountains, 'Fall on us,' and to the hills, 'Cover us.' For if they do this when the wood is green, what will happen when it is dry?"
>
> Luke 23:26-31

Never Alone

Standing out from the crowd of passersby, Simon of Cyrene became an unexpected companion to Jesus in his suffering, but not only Simon, these wailing women as well. In a moment of honesty, Jesus shared with the women just what he thought was happening and even about to happen, "Do not weep for me, but weep for yourselves and for your children." Sometimes we glaze over the words of Jesus, but I wonder if this, too, is an invitation into his suffering. Together Simon and the women stepped into one of the most sacred and agonizing journeys in history. Simon shouldered a weight that was not his to carry and these women a grief that declared Jesus was beloved. Together they stepped into the suffering of another, and in doing so, ensured that Jesus did not suffer alone. In that moment, Simon and the women embodied what it means to walk alongside another in pain, not with the intent to fix pain, not to remove suffering, but simply to be present.

Recently, I watched a TED Talk by Jason Brian Rosenthal, the widower of Amy Krouse Rosenthal. Amy wrote the heartbreakingly beautiful *New York Times* piece *You May Want to Marry My Husband*. If you decide to read the article, grab your tissues. In his talk, Jason walked listeners through the grueling last months and weeks of Amy's life as she battled ovarian cancer. As I listened, I was struck not just by the depth of his loss but by his profound gift of presence. Amy did not suffer alone. She was surrounded by love. There were people who held her hand, others who bore witness to her pain, and all ensured that she was accompanied through the end of her life. She was not alone. And is that not what we all long for? Not that suffering would never come, because suffering will. Suffering is the residue of being human. But rather that when suffering does come, we would not bear it in isolation.

Jesus, too, was surrounded in his final moments. There were those who mocked him, but there were those who loved him. The women, the female disciples, were there, mourning his suffering and refusing to look away. When nearly all the male disciples fled, these women remained. They followed Jesus and Simon weeping, watching, and grieving. And as Jesus walked toward the cross, "a great number of the people followed him, and among them were women who were beating their breasts and wailing for him" (Luke 23:27). They could not carry the weight of the cross for him, but they carried the pain of his suffering. Even in anguish, Jesus was not alone.

And neither are we. We are not alone. No one escapes suffering in this life; but what makes the difference is whether we suffer in isolation or in the presence of love. Simon of Cyrene carried the cross. The women wept at Jesus's feet. Jesus may have been crucified, but he was never unaccompanied. As we walk through our own seasons of grief, hardship, or uncertainty, we, too, are called to carry the burdens of others. We carry one another's burden not to fix one another. We are not qualified to solve one another's problems most of the time, but we can simply be present to ensure that no one suffers alone.

In the spring of 2023, New Albany United Methodist Church partnered with Horizon Stewardship to work on a capital campaign. Joe Park, CEO of Horizon, connected with us on our stewardship journey. I had been a friend and colleague of Joe for several years. In September 2023, he traveled from Dallas, Texas, to spend time in the home of our campaign chairs to talk with potential givers. Although Joe and I were scheduled to give that talk together, my mom landed in the hospital for the last time in her journey. Joe stepped in and in partnership with the testimony of the campaign chairs, led the entire meeting in my stead. I was grateful, but Joe's generosity did not stop there. He decided that before he caught a plane back to Dallas, he would travel to the hospital to pray with my momma. My family had never met Joe Park, and my younger sister Julie was struck by his soothing voice. His slow Arkansas accent took her by surprise. "Could I record you reading a story to my first-grade class?" she asked with a smile. She knew his voice alone would calm her rowdy bunch of students. Joe merely laughed. Not only did he bring words of encouragement to my mom and our family, but he earnestly prayed over my mother. We knew this was the beginning of the end, but we also knew we were not alone.

We need people. Particularly when walking through the valley of the shadow of death. It is often difficult to let people in during those times. I understand. I have this habit of not letting people see me sweat. I do not want to be a burden. It would be crushing for me to discover someone thought that I was needy, but I recognize my deep need for people.

There is a strange tension between independence and intimacy, between appearing strong and actually being supported. Sometimes I wonder if I have mistaken self-preservation for strength. The truth is, trying to carry grief, stress, or sorrow alone does not make me resilient; it makes me isolated. And isolation is a lonely echo chamber that often turns pain inward. What I long for is someone to sit beside me. I want others to hold space when words do not come. I need people to offer presence over performance. Just to be there. That kind of companionship is holy.

It has taken me a minute, but I am learning that vulnerability is not weakness. Vulnerability is a doorway to connection. It is okay to let others see the cracks in the walls I place between me and pain. Vulnerability invites people to show up with their whole selves too. The exchange is a holy reciprocity, a gentle reminder that we were never meant to walk this road alone. In those valley moments, when shadows feel longer than light, I am trying to remind myself that letting people in is not a burden. It's a blessing. It is okay to need others. In fact, needing others is deeply human.

In his book *Cherished Belonging*, Father Gregory Boyle reminds us that humans are unshakably good, no exceptions, and that we belong to one another, also no exceptions. Perhaps human suffering is what gifts us with a picture of being ever connected to one another in this woven tapestry we call life. We are always connected to one another.

Unlikely Companion

Although Simon of Cyrene was an unlikely companion for Jesus, perhaps suffering itself is the most unlikely companion of them all. Suffering is not something we ask for and it is an ever-present reality in our human experience.

I will never forget just days before my mom took her last breath, she insisted on participating in my morning prayer time on Facebook. It always makes me laugh a little. For years my mom chastised my participation on Facebook. "Social media is from the devil," she would exclaim. She could be passionate at times, particularly with regard to her opinions concerning social ills. "I will never be on Facebook!" I was attempting to convince my mom to start an account because I wanted her to see all the pictures we posted of her grandchildren. "You could just text me the pictures," she readily responded. I am sure I rolled my eyes at her on more than one occasion. Eventually she relented and started an account and soon she became a Facebook warrior. This Facebook opponent began to encourage everyone she ever met online. People she knew and people she did not know. My mother never quite understood how social media really worked. I cannot count the times she would say to me, "Rachel, so-and-so sent me pictures today." "Well, Mom," I would comment back, "those are merely on their timeline." It did not matter, my mom was determined to cheer and celebrate friends of friends of friends simply because a need presented itself on her screen. There was not a bigger-hearted people-champion on the planet.

So that particular morning mom smiled as I read through those familiar words of *Common Prayer: A Liturgy for Ordinary Radicals*, "O Lord, let my soul rise up to meet you / as the day rises to meet the sun."[1] And when it came time to sing, I asked, "Mom, what do you want to sing?" I know the book has a daily suggestion, but instead of giving me a title she just began softly singing, "Our God is an awesome God, / He reigns from heaven above." Suddenly, warm tears began to stream down my face. I could not quite grasp what was happening. I did not understand how this woman could be singing that song. How could a woman with a headwrap in place of hair, a bedsheet swaddling her rail-thin body, a warrior who was actively suffering and close to death by a horrific form of cancer sing that God is awesome? The sobs were overwhelming. It took a minute to get myself back together to pray. In the middle of my crisis, my mother was just smiling. Her face was full of joy. Once we had ended our live prayer time, I asked her why she chose that song. "Mom, what is it that prompted you to sing 'Our God Is an Awesome God'?" She thought about it for just a moment and declared, "Rachel, it took me back to those days when I helped you and your brother in youth group. Do you remember all of the concerts, campouts, youth group meetings, and even those moments when people were led to faith in Jesus?" We began to remember all that had taken place. My mom was always there, doing whatever she could to help her kids, but also other kids in the church grow in their faith in Jesus. I could not help thinking, there is a divine mystery to this faith we hold so dear. Songs sung together in human gatherings, youth group outings, plays, and Bible studies all bind us together in this dance we call life.

Let me be clear, I did not want my mom to suffer. And I certainly do not wish suffering on anyone, but I also recognize that those of us who call ourselves Christians follow a suffering Savior. So could it be that suffering is part of the program, part of being human? And might it be true that suffering is more than awkward emotions to be endured? Suffering is more than pain to be avoided. Could suffering be a pathway to growth, to life, and ultimately into love? Our culture tempts us with a message to avoid pain at all costs. And humans are certainly tempted to medicate it, distract from it, and silence it, but Jesus did not avoid suffering. He walked through it, and in doing so, he showed us that suffering is not the end of the story. What if, instead of running from our pain, we allowed it to shape us? What if we, like Simon, carried our pain not as a burden to break us, but as a companion to teach us?

Perhaps you, too, have a moment of suffering, past or present, that you have been avoiding. You do not talk about it. You do not want to think about it. But the pain and suffering always linger just beneath the surface of nearly every thought and conversation you have. Perhaps it is time to take a different approach. Instead of numbing or ignoring your pain, what would it look like to sit with it? Could you name your pain? Reader, this is really difficult for me to do as well. I want people to think I am strong and tough as nails. But we have a treasure in the church that we call lament: speaking truth to the pain we experience in our everyday lives. Instead of being quick to put on a happy face, sprint through the discomfort, or to merely get over it, what if you took time to grieve it? I have prayed these words of Jesus over more than one of the circumstances in my life,

> *"Father, if you are willing, remove this cup from me, yet not my will but yours be done."*
>
> *Luke 22:42*

Maybe you resemble me with my tendencies to minimize what I have gone through by saying things like "at least the situation is not as bad as so-and-so's situation" or "I have a lot to be grateful for." Instead hover over the pain and suffering you have endured. Let yourself feel what you have been afraid to feel. Are you disappointed? Perhaps you are even angry. There are moments when we are angry at God. The psalmists gave us ample permission to share with the Divine the myriad of emotions that we are carrying in our heads and our hearts:

> *How long, O Lord? Will you forget me forever?*
> *How long will you hide your face from me?*
> *How long must I bear pain in my soul*
> *and have sorrow in my heart all day long?*
>
> *Psalm 13:1-2a*

And when ready, like Simon of Cyrene, step forward and carry it, but do not carry it alone. Share your pain with someone you trust. Ask for prayer and seek community. Because while suffering may be part of the human experience, isolation does not have to be. We were designed to be in deep relationship with one another. Walk with it and more important, let others walk with you. Who knows? On the other side of suffering, you may discover resurrection waiting.

Practice: Sharing in One Another's Suffering

There are certainly moments in life when we whisper, "I didn't sign up for this." Moments when the weight of suffering is too much, the grief is too sharp, and the diagnosis is too real. But here is the truth: we do not walk this road alone. As Simon stepped in beside Jesus, we step in beside one another. Perhaps in this practice you could create holy space for yourself, individuals, or even the congregation to share in one another's suffering. Whether you place a single candle on a table or multiple tea lights on multiple tables, create a time for people to reflect on their own grief. Invite people to come forward and light a candle. Some will light the candle for the suffering and pain they themselves are carrying. Others will light the candle for someone else. Be sure to remind participants that the light is a sign that none of us suffer in isolation. When we witness multiple flames glowing during a rough moment in our lives, we realize we are not alone. I would encourage you to have leaders to pray with people if needed and necessary. I always encourage people to find help when deep in grief.

God of compassion, in our suffering and in our pain, you are near. Thank you for the gift of one another, for unlikely companions and the steady presence of love. May these small lights remind us that even in the darkest moments of our lives, your grace still shines. Amen.

Chapter 5
UNLIKELY
COURAGE
The Women at the Cross

Many women were also there, looking on from a distance; they had followed Jesus from Galilee, ministering to him. Among them were Mary Magdalene, and Mary the mother of James and Joseph, and the mother of the sons of Zebedee.

Matthew 27:55-56

I grew up in a "standard" United Methodist church in rural southeastern Ohio. A fire in the 1970s required the congregation to completely reconstruct the original church building. It is no surprise that copious amounts of wood paneling were the decor du jour. Two sections of padded pews formed a single aisle for the preacher, the choir, or even the occasional bride and groom to parade through the center of the church. The slightly out-of-tune piano was played by ear with untrained fingers. The small country church is and always will be my spiritual home. I also found a measure of comfort in gazing at the print of Jesus at the front of the church. Its frame was thick, wooden, simple, and certainly not gaudy. Within the frame was a fair-skinned Warner Sallman version of Jesus of Nazareth. The artist's rendering reflected the skin tones of the folks sitting in the pews. As a child I was drawn to the print, and I certainly did not question the artist's intent. Jesus seemed nice, safe, and not the kind of adult who was going to lay into you for lighting stuff on fire when you were serving as an acolyte, just as an example. Warner Sallman's Jesus seemed like the kind of emotionally reasonable adult who would take you to the side and help you understand the dangers of fires without twenty-five sets of adult eyes and ears witnessing the reprimand, you know, for all the world to see and hear. And about the time I ventured off to college, some leaders in the church decided to replace that print of Jesus with a gold cross. True confessions: I hated it at first because I love images of Jesus. Art speaks to me no matter the medium, but I did not love that metallic change. Of course, I love change as long as change is my idea. When other people decide to make changes without my input, I struggle. Perhaps you have had this experience a time or two in your life as well. As I wrestled with the inevitability of the change from beloved portrait to cold cross, I realized that the cross really has served as a marker of the faith from the beginnings of Christianity.

For All the World to See

From paintings to crypts, crosses have been used as distinguishing marks of people of The Way. Today many people place crosses on T-shirts to bow ties and nearly everything in-between. I, too, have a collection of crosses that I have picked up in my travels throughout the United States and the globe. A cross collection is kind of quirky when you think about it. The cross was a Roman tool of execution. It was a weapon at best and the electric chair at worst. The Romans used the cross not merely to kill people for their rebellion against Roman rule, but also to shame the victim and his followers. A sign of complete humiliation, the Roman cross was positioned along highly traveled roadways allowing those being crucified to serve as gruesome billboards. Its message read: "mess with Rome in the wrong way and this fate awaits you." To make matters even more horrifying, especially for first-century Jews, victims were crucified naked, intentionally shaming the crucified and anyone associated with said person. Jesus was not merely crucified as a common criminal; there were other means of punishment that could have done that job: imprisonment, flogging, or starvation just to name a few. But instead, the Romans chose to place the rebel Jesus on full display for all the world to see his humiliation.

Have you ever had a situation when you felt like your whole life was on full display for all the world to see? Social media makes that more probable for the average human. Public humiliation used to be limited to the infamous. If a person was wealthy enough or powerful enough, or if the crime one was accused of was horrific enough, his or her story might make it into the newspaper or heaven forbid, the nightly news. But today smear campaigns travel faster than the speed of light. So-called regular folks have their lives flipped upside down because of the invention of the share button. I have walked and talked with several people whose painful news went viral for all the wrong reasons. Suddenly, something that would have been limited to the neighborhood gossip becomes a national affair. It is terrifying and leaves many feeling like their reputations, their careers, and their very lives have been broken beyond repair. And in those moments these folks are grasping for any way to get back to normal.

Craving Comfort

Craving comfort is where we find the disciples. They have watched their fearless leader be arrested, tried, and led to the outskirts of Jerusalem to be crucified. Most of the disciples have scattered and who can blame them? These men have invested years of their lives, perhaps even their most productive years, into this would-be street preacher and now their decisions are on full display for all the world to see. They are grasping for any semblance of safe normalcy. Humans in general are fairly addicted to comfort. When life gets hard, when the news is bad, when stepping out seems way too risky, we just want to hide and heal. We avoid becoming part of the scene. We crave our comfort, arranging our lives around the safety and security of the familiar. We cling to what feels safe and predictable, whether that's the soft recliner in the living room, the expected routine of our days, or our own circle of people who won't challenge our thinking. We avoid stepping out into unknown territory.

Have you ever been in a situation where you wondered if you should get involved? Perhaps it was that moment in high school when two students were fighting and everyone else was just standing around watching, and you thought to yourself someone should do something about this. Or the moment when the boss reprimanded the wrong employee for the mistake, and you just kept quiet. Perhaps on more than one occasion you noticed a person in distress at the grocery store, and you quickly turned down a different aisle. There are so many times I have witnessed someone pulled off on the side of the road in need of assistance, and I began rehearsing all the reasons why I should not stop and help. We have all kinds of legitimate excuses for choosing not to get involved, but the storyteller Matthew records an unlikely courage coming from an unlikely place:

> *Many women were also there, looking on from a distance; they had followed Jesus from Galilee, ministering to him. Among them were Mary Magdalene, and Mary the mother of James and Joseph, and the mother of the sons of Zebedee.*
>
> *Matthew 27:55-56*

In the final moments of Jesus's life, courage emerged among the women at the cross. While the male disciples apparently fled in fear, these women stayed. They did not run; they did not hide; but instead bore witness to the suffering of Jesus. Their presence was not incidental. Their presence was intentional. The phrase "had followed," used in reference to these women, is language that signals discipleship.[1] These women were not merely passive observers; they were followers of Jesus in every sense of the word. Each one of the Gospel writers mentions these women at the Crucifixion.

> *And when all the crowds who had gathered there for this spectacle saw what had taken place, they returned home, beating their breasts. But all his acquaintances, including the women who had followed him from Galilee, stood at a distance watching these things.*
>
> *Luke 23:48-49*

> *There were also women looking on from a distance. Among them were Mary Magdalene, and Mary the mother of James the younger and of Joses, and Salome, who followed him when he was in Galilee and ministered to him, and there were many other women who had come up with him to Jerusalem.*
>
> Mark 15:40-41

While Luke softened the statement by including men at the cross, Mark's Gospel presented a stark absence of male disciples, highlighting the women's courage all the more. Some scholars have nearly ignored these women, skimming over their presence as though it has no bearing on the Gospels. Some commentators have been quick to dismiss their mention, but the reality is, the presence of these women changes everything we think about faith in Jesus. While the surrounding social circles saw them as insignificant, the Gospel place them front and center as the ones who remained faithful.

It is true that women were generally perceived as less of a threat to Rome than men, but this would not dismiss these women's complete disregard for their own safety and security. They were followers of Jesus, and their courageous journey led them all the way to the cross. Mary Magdalene held prominence in these accounts. Her name appeared first in the lists of women both at the cross and the tomb. Each of the Gospel accounts records a different list of names for the women accompanying Jesus at both places. Could there have been dozens of women hanging around Jesus? Did someone not pen the correct list? Or perhaps, over the hours of witnessing this form of capital punishment, from the hammering of that first nail up through Jesus's final breath, might these women have set up an entire rotation, a brigade of care for the moments that Jesus needed them the most?

A brigade of faith-filled women is not a stretch for me to imagine. I have experienced numerous groups of women who rallied around folks in need from meal trains during a season of loss to an entire list of caregivers when a child goes through a major health crisis. Women have a way of organizing themselves to get stuff done.

As an extreme extrovert, I knew I would need people around me. Although I had grandparents eager to help, they would not be able to be by my side while making my way through the first few months of my eldest child's life. I established a rotation where more seasoned women from Duke's Chapel United Methodist Church would come and visit AJ and myself. Once a week they would bring dinner for our new trio. They always stayed to hold the new baby. This group of women were strong members of what was then known as the United Methodist Women's group in our church. Today, United Women in Faith have a long history of caring for those in need. It all began in 1869 when a group of eight women in Boston decided to step out in faith.[2] There was an urgent need to help women in India with health care and education. From these eight women, the Methodist Woman's Foreign Missionary Society was established. These women of faith began a ministry that would focus on women, children, education, and advocacy. I can still remember the library that the United Methodist Women at Duke's Chapel formed to keep the entire congregation educated, particularly when it came to human suffering and social justice.

It was no wonder I loved talking with these women. They did more than talk about faith in Jesus. They lived faith out. When needs arose in the community, they met those needs. Whether it was visiting their seminary intern after the birth of her first child or throwing a birthday party for kids at the local homeless shelter, these women were eager to use their gifts and talents to serve Jesus and people.

If you have been part of a faith community for any length of time, perhaps you, too, have experienced the care of a group of women ready to serve you in your time of need. I could share numerous stories of women stepping up and out in faith to ensure people are cared for and they have what they need. Certainly, my experience in the church also has included men who have made meals, baked cookies, and even offered to care for my children in times of need. And yet I have discovered that women continue to have a knack for organizing themselves, especially when life is really challenging.

> *There were also women looking on from a distance. Among them were Mary Magdalene, and Mary the mother of James the younger and of Joses, and Salome, who followed him when he was in Galilee and ministered to him, and there were many other women who had come up with him to Jerusalem.*
>
> *Mark 15:40-41*

Who were these women at the cross? And why were they present? Though some traditions associate Salome with the sons of Zebedee, she is not explicitly identified here in Mark by her family ties. Why? Mark's description of Salome was such a contrast to how women were often referenced in patriarchal genealogies. The Gospel writer recognized her for who she was, not for whose wife or mother she might have been. I want to hover over this for a moment. Mark was saying here that Salome, a disciple of Jesus, was someone who cared for Jesus and his traveling ministry while he was in Jerusalem.

I have grown particularly fond of the television series *The Chosen*. Although creator and cowriter Dallas Jenkins takes artistic liberties in the film and emphasizes particular aspects of Christian theology that I do not agree with, overall, the portrayal of Jesus and the disciples is beautiful. I am intrigued by Jenkins's portrayal of the women surrounding Jesus. Jesus empowered women from the very beginning of his ministry. I will not spoil the entire plot for you, but Mary of Magdala was one of the first of the disciples chosen to follow Jesus. These women are not merely sidekicks to the story of Jesus but rather take prominent roles through the series. Although I believe Jenkins challenges many assumptions concerning these female disciples, he like many in the past tends to meld many female disciples and their identities together. For example, Salome was portrayed as the wife of Zebedee and mother to James and John. Jenkins and his writers assumed that Mary of Magdala had a scandalous past. This practice is not new. Over time, these women and their identities have been conflated in tradition. Perhaps this was an attempt to make these women easier to categorize. But their individuality matters, and their courage is vitally important.

It is not every day that women had the freedom to travel with a nomadic teacher. Women, particularly those of childbearing age, would have been expected to attend to domestic life. It seemed odd, perhaps even shocking, that some of these women would have been publicly supporting Jesus and his ministry. Jesus championed women.

We live in a time and culture, particularly those in the United States, where Christian Nationalists are questioning the role of women in the church. Recently I listened to a clip from a podcast where a group of Christian Nationalist podcasters were advocating for the United States government to seize the property of churches who ordain women as clergy and display pride flags. As an ordained elder of The United Methodist Church, this kind of rhetoric is alarming but not surprising. For centuries Christians have debated the presence and role of women in the church. There is a rise of complementarian theology, particularly among Christian Nationalists. Complementarian theology in its simplest form is an understanding of God's creation of women and their to purpose is support, that is, to complement men in the world. Therefore, women are relegated to domestic life and the raising of children and families.

The conversation has become mainstream. We witness this understanding of men and women play out in moments of public discourse. For example, Kansas City Chiefs kicker Harrison Butker made such remarks in his commencement address at Benedictine College. In front of young graduates with bright futures ahead, he said to the women graduating, "Some of you may go on to lead successful careers in the world. But I would venture to guess that the majority of you are most excited about your marriage and the children you will bring into this world."[3] His words hit a nerve. For some listening, Butker's remarks felt like a throwback to a world where women's worth was tied to the home and men's to leadership. And for others, his remarks reflected the kind of traditional values they want to preserve. But Jesus did not limit women in the way that Butker was prescribing. Jesus championed women and men to live into the full vibrant picture of God's calling. Jesus certainly did not box women into their domestic roles, but rather Jesus unleashed them to lead, serve, create, and live out a calling that was bigger than any societal role.

Jesus opened many doors of possibility for women. He championed the Samaritan woman at the well, empowering her to be his first evangelist. "Many Samaritans from that city believed in him because of the woman's testimony, 'He told me everything I have ever done.' So when the Samaritans came to him, they asked him to stay with them, and he stayed there two days" (John 4:39-40).

A Canaanite woman called Jesus to the carpet. She was an outsider and desperate for her daughter to be healed. Jesus did not reject her, but rather commended her for her faith, "'Woman, great is your faith! Let it be done for you as you wish.'" And her daughter was healed from that moment" (Matthew 15:28).

It is hard for me to imagine someone who reads through the New Testament and disregards Jesus's treatment of women. Although many times these women are unnamed, they are penned as examples of courageous faith. So why do people attempt to relegate women to the religious sidelines? Is it fear? Is it ignorance? Is it anger? I firmly believe when we limit the role of women in the church, we limit the roles of everyone in the church.

In contrast to complementarian theology is egalitarian theology. Egalitarian theology, I believe, is the heartbeat of the gospel. It is the belief that every single person is created equal in value, dignity, and worth before God. From the very beginning, God's story shows us this truth that every human reflects the *imago Dei*, the image of God, "So God created humans in his image, in the image of God he created them; male and female he created them" (Genesis 1:27). We are made in the image of

God. *Imago Dei* is not a spiritual soundbite. It is a declaration that cuts through every human-made boundary. No matter where you come from, who you are, or how the world tries to categorize you, you carry the divine imprint of God's creativity and purpose. Women matter to God, because all human beings matter to God.

Have you ever had an experience where someone attempted to limit your participation in the church? Perhaps it was because of where you grew up, your family of origin, your race, your primary language, or any other limiting factor. I call these moments in our lives "limitation prophecies." They are moments in our lives when others have said "you can't, you shouldn't, and you won't." These limitation prophecies have real consequences to the way we perceive ourselves and others. Many people of all genders have grown up limiting their role in the church because of what someone has said about their identity. And I challenge our perception of that reality, considering Jesus's empowerment of women. His interaction is not merely about the women. He was breaking down barriers and giving us a fuller picture of the kingdom of God.

Perhaps it is time for us to reevaluate the limits we have placed on ourselves or others. What would it look like for you to reimagine faith and faithfulness in light of Jesus's treatment of women? What persons or even groups of people have you placed outside of the grace of God? Could it be that Jesus is calling you to erase the lines and breakdown the barriers you've drawn and held so dear?

I cannot conclude discussing the women at the cross without turning your attention to Jesus's final interaction with his mother and the beloved disciple, John.

Meanwhile, standing near the cross of Jesus were his mother, and his mother's sister, Mary the wife of Clopas, and Mary Magdalene. When Jesus saw his mother and the disciple whom he loved standing beside her, he said to his mother, "Woman, here is your son." Then he said to the disciple, "Here is your mother." And from that hour the disciple took her into his own home.

John 19:25-27

If the male disciples were in danger of being arrested, how could the beloved disciple get away with being at the foot of the cross? Would this not have been a death sentence for John? Some scholars, like N. T. Wright, suggest that "the disciple whom Jesus loved" may have been very young, perhaps too young to be perceived as a threat. Imagine with me the beloved is actually a teenager, and although he was eager to follow Jesus, he had not yet grown a beard.[4] Could it be that he had not hit a growth spurt? What if his youthfulness kept him out of trouble? This detail shifts our understanding of who remained at the cross. Those who stayed with Jesus were those the world would most likely overlook. These were the young ones, the supposedly weak ones. The people at the cross were the ones not seen as dangerous. Yet, they were the ones who displayed the greatest courage. Even when the surrounding culture dismissed them, these were the ones who refused to turn away. They stood firm in love, in grief, and in faith.

In a moment where fear consumed even the strongest of men, it was chiefly the young ones and the women who remained. Their courage, their devotion, and their discipleship stand as a testimony that God often works through the unlikely. While history may try to forget them, especially the women, the gospel does not and neither should we. Perhaps this is a faith that was not rooted in position or in power, but deeply rooted in relationship.

A Different Kind of Faith

These women followed Jesus not because he gave them influence or authority, but because they loved him. Their faith wasn't transactional; it was not about what they could gain. It was personal, deeply woven into their daily lives. For these women, staying at the cross was not a question of strategy or safety; staying with Jesus was the only action that made sense. They had walked with him, learned from him, and been transformed by Jesus. Where else would they go?

This was not a faith that weighed risks or calculated benefits. It was the kind of faith that could not be dragged away by fear, by scandal, or by the violence of the cross. These women refused to turn away because their relationship with Jesus was embedded in their hearts and their lives. He was their first thought in the morning, the one who had given them hope, dignity, and purpose. To abandon Jesus in his suffering would have been to abandon themselves and the lives they now embodied. Leaving him would have been unthinkable. They were not trying to prove anything to the world. These women simply loved him too much to leave. I am not advocating for some kind of sentimentality, but rather a love that is costly.

And Jesus, even in his dying moments, modeled this same relational faith. As he hung on the cross, he looked at his mother and the beloved disciple and told them to care for each other. In that moment, Jesus established a new kind of family. The new family was not based on blood, but on love, faithfulness, and commitment. Jesus's words were not merely for Mary and the beloved disciple, but rather his words were for all of us. The church is meant to be this kind of community. We are a people bound together not by DNA, status, or power, but by the deep, abiding love of Christ. We perceive ourselves as belonging to one another, caring for one another, forever bound together in faith. Mary and John serve as a prototype of this kind of family and community.

Sometimes it is difficult, in our "my four and no more," Western-culture-understanding of the family unit, to fully grasp what it means to be part of the body of Christ and the family of God. Perhaps one of the simplest declarations are the commitments we make when we baptize persons of all ages. In my faith tradition we commit:

> With God's help we will proclaim the good news and live according to the example of Christ. We will surround these persons with a community of love and forgiveness, that they may grow in their trust of God, and be found faithful in their service to others. We will pray for them, that they may be true disciples who walk in the way that leads to life.[5]

Even on the cross, Jesus was advocating for a new way to be family, a new way to form community. And these women at the cross show us what it looks like to follow Jesus with a faith rooted in relationship. They remind us that discipleship is not about who holds the microphone or who gets the recognition. Discipleship is about showing up, staying close, and loving Jesus with a devotion that refuses to turn away. It is a different kind of faith, a faith of one who stays with Jesus, no matter the cost.

Following Jesus means we show up for one another, both when life falls apart and when life overflows with joy. It looks like bringing a casserole when someone's world shatters and baking a plateful of cookies when there is a milestone to celebrate. But discipleship is more than just caring for our friends. Discipleship is about ensuring that those who are experiencing food insecurity have something to eat. It is standing beside the stranger who needs protection. Discipleship is about making space for the immigrant family terrified of a knock at the door. It's advocating for the LGBTQ+ student who just wants to be safe at school. It means championing the gifted child who needs someone to fight for their right to thrive. Walking alongside one another means seeing people the way Jesus does, not as problems to be solved, but as beloveds to be supported. It means saying, "I'm with you," not just in words but with our very presence, in action, and in love. Because showing up was exactly what Jesus did, and being present is what you and I are called to do. But, Reader, let me be honest, sometimes following Jesus is costly.

I will never forget the first time I read about Clarence Jordan. It was not merely an assignment for ethics class. Reading Stanley Hauerwas's *The Interpretation of Scripture: Why Discipleship Is Required* was a wake-up call. Clarence Jordan's different kind of faith cut me to the core because it was not just about what he believed; it was about what he was willing to lose for the gospel. Clarence was more than just a New Testament scholar. He was a farmer. This farmer had the audacity to take Jesus at his word. In the 1940s, he founded Koinonia Farm in southwest Georgia, a community rooted in radical discipleship where Black and white people lived and worked together as equals. *Koinonia* is a Greek word meaning communion or fellowship. Koinonia was not merely an ideal for Clarence; it was a way of life. At first, the neighbors did not mind this alternative family and faith community he had created. But when the civil rights movement gained momentum, the community's very existence became a threat. The cost of following Jesus got real.

By the late 1950s, Koinonia was under siege. Businesses refused to sell to them. Gas companies, breaking the law, refused to deliver fuel in the winter. Their roadside produce stand was riddled with bullets. The cost of discipleship was not theoretical; they were attempting to survive. When their situation grew worse, Clarence turned to his brother Robert, a rising politician, and asked him to represent Koinonia in court. Robert hesitated. "Clarence, I can't do that. You know my political aspirations. If I represent you, I might lose my job, my house, everything I've got." Clarence's response was simple and devastating: "We might lose everything too, Bob." Robert pushed back, "It's different for you." But Clarence wasn't having it. "Why is it different?…you and I joined the church on the same Sunday, as boys. I expect when we came forward the preacher asked me about the same question he did you: 'Do you accept Jesus as your Lord and Savior?' I said yes. What did you say?" Robert sighed, "I follow Jesus, Clarence, but up to a point." Clarence leaned in, "Could that point by any chance be—the cross?" Robert nodded, "That's right. I follow him to the cross, but not *on* the cross. I'm not getting myself crucified." And Clarence, in the way only he could, said, "Then I don't believe you're a disciple. You're an admirer of Jesus, but not a disciple of his. I think you ought to go back to the church you belong to, and tell them you're an admirer, not a disciple." Robert shot back,

"Well now, if everyone who felt like I do did that, we wouldn't have a church, would we?" Clarence let the question hang in the air. "The question," Clarence said, is "Do you have a church?"[6]

Clarence reminded his brother Robert, and you and me, that being the church means something. The cost of following Jesus is not limited to what we say we believe. Following Jesus is about what we are willing to lose. For Clarence that cost was tangible: opposition, threats, and poverty. Sometimes when we read stories like this one it is easy to come up with all kinds of excuses. But Clarence knew the truth that the gospel was never meant to be comfortable. It was always destined to be costly.

Courageously Follow Jesus

As Jesus hung on the cross, most of his followers had scattered. Gripped by fear they had fled to the shadows, unwilling to risk their lives for the man they once called Lord. But not the women. Mary Magdalene, Mary the mother of Jesus, Mary the mother of Joseph and Joses, Mary the wife of Clopas, and Salome, stood at the foot of the cross, refusing to turn away. They had followed Jesus not just when it was easy. There were easier times, when the crowds gathered and the miracles flowed, but these women followed when it cost them everything. Their presence at the cross was an act of defiance against fear, a declaration that their love for Jesus was greater than their need for safety. They did not just admire him when he was healing the sick and raising the dead; they risked following him all the way to suffering, to sorrow, to the place where hope seemed lost.

The women at the cross show us what faithful discipleship looks like. They did not know what would happen next. They did not have the luxury of hindsight, the promise of resurrection fully realized. These women do not live on our side of history, and yet they stood firm, hearts broken but faith intact, refusing to abandon the one who had never abandoned them. The courage of these women stands as a challenge to us today. It is one thing to follow Jesus when it costs us little, when faith is convenient and respectable. But when the weight of the cross becomes real, when discipleship asks us to stand in uncomfortable places, to speak out against injustice, to love when it is costly, what will we do then?

Are we admirers of Jesus, or are we ready to follow? Are we content to stand at a distance, agreeing with his teachings, enjoying the comfort of his words but shrinking back when the cross appears? Or will we, like these women, have the courage to stand with Jesus in the hard places, to follow him even when it costs us, to love him with courageous and unwavering devotion? The cross demands an answer. And the only way to resurrection is straight through it.

Practice: Committing to Following Jesus

There are many tangible ways that we can commit to following Jesus, not only with our words but also with our actions. We are invited to move beyond admiration and into action. Jesus never asked for admirers. He called disciples. Following Jesus means allowing our hearts to break for what breaks his, and then letting those broken pieces guide our hands and feet toward healing and justice.

When we look out into the world and whisper, "Someone should do something about that," perhaps Jesus is whispering back, "Yes. You." That gentle nudge is the Spirit calling us to step in. When we witness immigrant families living in fear, LGBTQ+ students who feel unseen or unsafe, children in our own neighborhoods going to school hungry, or seniors in isolation with no visitors, it is not merely just a tragedy, it is a call. Following Jesus means we stop waiting for others to fix what's broken and instead we partner with God to take up the work of restoration.

During worship, invite people to write down the burden that is stirring in their hearts: the injustice, the pain, the need they can no longer ignore. Write it on a card or sticky note. Have them name the place where they sense Jesus calling them to show up. Then invite them to come forward and nail it to the cross. It is not about guilting anyone into action; this is about receiving God's grace. In this action we are saying, "Jesus, I will go where you go. I will follow, even when it is hard, even when it costs me."

This is our holy moment of courage. The cross is not just a symbol of suffering; it is the place where our commitments become real. This act does not mean people will have all the answers or even all the courage they need. But it does mean they are committed to start. And sometimes the most powerful faith begins when people simply say, "I'm willing." Invite them to bring their commitments forward and nail them to the cross, perhaps this will be a milestone in their faith journey as they move from admiring Jesus to courageously following him with their whole lives.

Jesus, the struggle is real. We crave comfort and security when life gets tough. Give us the strength to help one another follow the example of these courageous women and commit ourselves to follow you no matter what the cost. And remind us that we are in this work together. Amen.

Chapter 6
UNLIKELY ALLIES
Joseph of Arimathea and Nicodemus

After these things, Joseph of Arimathea, who was a disciple of Jesus, though a secret one because of his fear of the Jews, asked Pilate to let him take away the body of Jesus. Pilate gave him permission, so he came and removed his body. Nicodemus, who had at first come to Jesus by night, also came, bringing a mixture of myrrh and aloes, weighing about a hundred pounds.

John 19:38-39

Signs of spring are everywhere: trees blooming, flowers blossoming, and rain saturating the ground. The season of brown is giving way to a sea of green. And on a great day in central Ohio the sun will shine once again! Resurrection is all around us, and yet on Palm Sunday we are reminded that life is not always as it seems. There are moments in our world when we feel the crowds cheering, people celebrating, declaring, "Hosanna!

Blessed is the one who comes in the name of the Lord—the King of Israel!" (John 12:13). There is hope, there is joy, there is a future world order that seems possible. Much like those folks in the first century, it does not take us humans long to turn those hosannas into "Crucify him! Crucify him!" The atmosphere was tense, the future was uncertain, and those in power seemed to be disconnected from regular people. Reader, let me remind you that I am describing people in first-century Jerusalem. Under the surface there was a deep desperation for political stability and an end to civil unrest among the people. We recognize there is the world as it is, and then there is a world as we dream it should be, and it is the gap that at times drives humanity to near madness.

Daryl Davis was no stranger to this gap. Born in Chicago in 1958, Davis spent his growing-up years as the son of a foreign diplomat. Because of his father's respected position, Davis was shielded from the racism of the 1960s experienced by many Black families in the United States. Although his father's career exposed Daryl to diverse experiences around the globe, it was after joining an all-white Scout troop in Massachusetts that Davis had an experience that would shape his future and his purpose. While marching with his Scout pack, carrying the American flag in a local parade, he was struck with rocks and bottles from people in the crowd. Immediately Davis's pack leaders formed a protective ring around him. Davis was thoroughly confused by the experience, and it was not until talking with his father that he realized he had experienced racism for the first time in his life. Daryl was ten years old. Fast-forward with me a few decades. Davis had become an accomplished pianist, and in 1983 was playing in what he termed "country and western white bar." After hearing Davis play, a local patron remarked, "I've never heard a black man play as well as

Jerry Lee Lewis." How did Davis respond? He decided to have a conversation with the man, explaining that Jerry Lee learned to play from one of his closest friends. The two decided to have a drink together and that was when the patron confessed he was a member of the Ku Klux Klan. For most people, that would be the end of the conversation. And rightfully so, because the conversation would not seem safe. But not for Daryl Davis. This moment was a crossroads for him, and he decided to make it his life's purpose to befriend members of the KKK. In his book *Klan-Destine Relationships*, Davis sought to answer the question, "How can someone hate me when he doesn't even know me?" Through his conversations, relationships, and anti-racism efforts, nearly two hundred ex-Klan members attribute their departure from the Klan to Daryl Davis. Many of them gave Davis their old Klan robes as a sign of their commitment to leave racism behind.

Unlikely Relationships

To say that Davis developed an unlikely relationship seems like a vast understatement. His courage and willingness to step into conversations with adversaries—and dare I say, enemies—seems contradictory to everything we know to be safe or wise. And yet fueled by his life experience and his commitment to Jesus, Davis was determined to "love his enemies." I imagine there are many of us who struggle to even think about having a conversation with someone who is opposed to our very existence. But could it be there is deep growth to be gained when confronting hate with love, meeting ignorance with calm conversation, and facing resistance with understanding? Davis sought to build empathy. He remarked of his conversations with enemies, "If you are talking, you are not fighting!" Could it be that these unlikely connections serve as the foundation to experiencing the world not as it is but as God would have it? It seems downright impossible to foster these reconciled relationships, doesn't it? How can this even happen? In our divisive world of talking heads and political pundits, unlikely relationships feel like a waste of time. Hate presents as a force that cannot be overcome. How, you might ask, can these relationships be fostered today?

I am a sucker for a good unlikely friendship story. You know, the kind where two people who have no business getting along somehow find a way to make a relationship work. Maybe it is a friendship with the grumpy neighbor down the street. Perhaps it's the neighbor who shouts when the kids cut through their yard. It is easy to dismiss that neighbor. We assume that the neighbor is just mean. But one day you stop and have a real conversation with that neighbor. You learn they are not angry at the kids. As you dive deeper into conversation, you discover they are simply frustrated with their aging body and their inability to do what they once could do. And suddenly, their anger does not seem so personal. You grab a rake, help with the yard, and before you know it, that cranky neighbor starts waving instead of scowling.

Or maybe the unlikely friendship is with that coworker who has always been your rival. The coworker who seems determined to outdo you at every turn. You have spent years dodging their competitive jabs and rolling your eyes when they talk. But then the day comes when you are both stuck in the office late, and they let something slip. They are struggling at home, an admission of loneliness. And in that moment, the competition fades. You realize they are not your enemy. They are just another human trying to do their best. An office conversation leads to understanding and understanding to an unexpected camaraderie.

And then there is that friend on social media, the one whose posts make your blood pressure rise. Yes, Reader, that one! You know they did not vote the way you voted. Their opinions could not be more different from yours, and you are very tempted to type out a response, hit send, and set the record straight. But then, something holds you back. Instead of firing off a comment, you send them a message: Hey, how are you? Let's grab coffee sometime. And when you gather for that cup of coffee, you talk about family, about work, and about regular life. That deeply rich and meaningful conversation reminds you why you were friends in the first place. Turns out, they are not just the sum of their political views. They are a person, a human being just like you.

Could it be that love—real inside-out take-the-first-step kind of love—has the power to transform enemies into friends, rivals into partners, and strangers into allies? Could it be that the people we are most likely to dismiss, the ones we assume are just "not our people," are the very ones God is calling us to know? When we engage in calm conversation, when we listen well and love regardless, something miraculous happens. We stop seeing each other as adversaries. We start seeing each other as human beings. In that work of reconciliation, we might just discover an unlikely ally.

Unlikely allies are who we find in the Gospel of John. Unlike any other Gospel writer, John partnered influential members of the Jewish ruling council, Joseph of Arimathea and Nicodemus together. Their combined purpose was to bury the crucified Jesus of Nazareth. Joseph of Arimathea was mentioned by each of the

Gospel authors, but John specifically added Nicodemus to the mix probably as a result of his theological agenda. Before we look at their pairing, it's important to read through the context that John established in his account of the Crucifixion.

> *Since it was the day of Preparation, the Jews did not want the bodies left on the cross during the Sabbath, especially because that Sabbath was a day of great solemnity. So they asked Pilate to have the legs of the crucified men broken and the bodies removed. Then the soldiers came and broke the legs of the first and of the other who had been crucified with him. But when they came to Jesus and saw that he was already dead, they did not break his legs. Instead, one of the soldiers pierced his side with a spear, and at once blood and water came out. (He who saw this has testified so that you also may believe. His testimony is true, and he knows that he tells the truth, so that you also may continue to believe.) These things occurred so that the scripture might be fulfilled, "None of his bones shall be broken." And again another passage of scripture says, "They will look on the one whom they have pierced." After these things, Joseph of Arimathea, who was a disciple of Jesus, though a secret one because of his fear of the Jews, asked Pilate to let him take away the body of Jesus. Pilate gave him permission, so he came and removed his body. Nicodemus, who had at first come to Jesus by night, also came, bringing a mixture of myrrh and aloes, weighing about a hundred pounds.*
>
> *John 19:31-39*

Everyday Obligations

Joseph and Nicodemus were both members of the Sanhedrin, the Jewish ruling council. The Sanhedrin comprised seventy men who served as the legal, legislative, and judicial body of Jewish people. Both Joseph of Arimathea and Nicodemus had vital roles to play in the community. There was not a distinction between religious and social categories in first-century Judaism; therefore, these men functioned as influencers of their day. Every morning, they rose before the sun and stepped into a rhythm of prayer, Scripture, and duty. They walked through the temple courts, their presence commanding respect, their words shaping the faith of those who gathered to listen to their interpretations of the law. They would have settled disputes, interpreted the law, and ensured the community remained faithful to the traditions of the Jewish faith. There was a whole lot of responsibility. And that vital responsibility greeted them each morning when they woke up. They carried this mantle of leadership with both poise, pride, and pressure. Joseph and Nicodemus had to know that their influence mattered.

By midday, their work was layered with decisions big and small. It reminds me of the moment that Jethro, Moses's father-in-law, witnessed Moses's duties among the people. Jethro saw the pressure Moses was under and declared, "What is this that you are doing for the people? Why do you sit alone, while all the people stand around you from morning until evening?" (Exodus 18:14). Although there were multiple leaders to hear the people and their concerns, these men would have been expected to serve a variety of roles in the community. Joseph might be asked to sit with other council members, debating the nuances of a legal matter, ensuring that justice was not merely a word but a practice. Nicodemus, on the other hand, could have been deep in conversation with a young student, explaining the intricacies of the Torah, helping him wrestle with the same questions he once had. These men were not just scholars; they were politicians and shepherds. They guided, they instructed, and they led. And yet, underneath all of the responsibility, these men were still humans who wondered, who questioned, who, despite all their knowledge, still found themselves searching for something more. As a religious leader, I have a deep empathy for the pressure that these men found themselves under.

Were they worried about what the influence of Rome was having on their faith community, on their families, on the next generation of young rabbis? Were these men weary because the expectations had increased over the years so that they were no longer merely adherents of the law, but rather dealing with the expectations that just kept piling up? Could it be that they, too, were expected to serve as healers, combat community challenges, and solve social ills? Some days I feel the pressure to be everything from a personal therapist (which I am not) to a company CEO and everything in between. The job description of a pastor has increased significantly in the last couple of decades. Humans have very high expectations for their religious leaders. The people wanted these men to do something about Rome, about the occupation, and about their experience of oppression.

Reader, you do not have to be a religious influencer to feel the pressure of everyday obligations. Perhaps you are a first-grade teacher who is expected to teach children to read while walking them through active shooter drills. As a nurse you have more responsibility than ever before. Of course you are expected to check charts, but now it's your responsibility to ensure that every medication is properly dosed, that your patients have access to social services, and to determine if your patient is experiencing any form of elder abuse. There are some of you who serve as attorneys who are caught up in numerous cases with many people who have no understanding of how the law even works. But they heard a lawyer say something on TikTok that one time and they are convinced they now understand the law. It is a growing frustration! Or maybe you are a tech guy or gal who feels the pressure to create the latest and greatest app. Many are parents who feel like even perfection is no longer perfect, and the expectation is now to be the end-all-be-all for your children. You must sign up for the school fundraiser, volunteer at the art show, and coach your kids' latest sport of choice. All of these are everyday obligations. We all feel the pressure of everyday obligations—at work, at home, in our community.

It is no wonder we struggle to slow our minds when we turn off the lights at night. There are bills to pay, mouths to feed, and futures to plan for. And I have not even talked about the news cycles or political pressures. Daily life can seem so overwhelming. It is not a stretch to assume that Joseph and Nicodemus may have been attempting to survive and to live out their calling. Maybe they did not want to rock the boat with regard to Rome.

The author of the Gospel of John mentions that Joseph of Arimathea "who was a disciple of Jesus, though a secret one because of his fear of the Jews, asked Pilate to let him take away the body of Jesus" (John 19:38). And in John 3 Nicodemus approached Jesus under the cover of night, perhaps not wanting to be seen with the likes of this street preacher:

> Now there was a Pharisee named Nicodemus, a leader of the Jews. He came to Jesus by night and said to him, "Rabbi, we know that you are a teacher who has come from God, for no one can do these signs that you do unless God is with that person."
> John 3:1-2

Nicodemus sought out Jesus, looking for answers to his many questions. Did he come to Jesus in the dark because he was embarrassed? Was Nicodemus avoiding being seen with Jesus of Nazareth, or did Nicodemus genuinely want individual access to have a private conversation with Jesus? Whereas other religious leaders perceived Jesus to be an adversary, Nicodemus had the courage to be curious and ask the hard questions. Joseph of Arimathea and Nicodemus both had questions. They were curious about the religious claims of this man. They followed Jesus, albeit at a distance. Could it be that regular life obligations had kept them from moving beyond this curiosity? Could it be they were husbands, maybe fathers, worried about putting their families at risk should they follow too close to this renegade Jesus? They experienced a degree of safety and security as members of the Sanhedrin. If they followed Jesus in his nomadic ministry, would it cost them their position, their livelihood, and their power?

Before we judge Joseph and Nicodemus too harshly, we must admit we have lived our fair share of cautious faith. And whether that caution was personal or part of the religion you grew up in, many people were taught that faith was a private matter. I grew up being told at dinner parties we do not talk about religion or politics. These men were religious professionals, and Jesus had to seem like a rebel, perhaps even an unpolished amateur. Would I, as a religious professional, be willing to follow a street preacher who gathered a group of tax collectors, fishermen, and women as his trusted students? Could I give up my Cadillac of benefits—health, housing, pension—to make this kind of bold move? Just the thought makes me throw up in my mouth a little bit! Perhaps I, too, should have grace and empathy for these religious power brokers of their day. Sometimes we want to follow Jesus. We just do not want following Jesus to be costly. Early in ministry, I remember my mentor, pastor Mike Slaughter, regularly reminded young leaders about the temptation we have as Christians to want Jesus to become part of our worldview rather than us adopting his kingdom worldview. It is life with a dash of Jesus.

It is tempting for humans like you and me, Nicodemus and Joseph, to be cautiously curious. The desire to follow Jesus, to be an authentic disciple, is there, but we struggle to assimilate our faith throughout life's obligations, challenges, and potential risks of outing our own beliefs.

Even as a pastor I occasionally find myself wondering if I should claim the term "Christian." Do not misunderstand what I am saying. I want to follow Jesus, but with all the harm that has been done in the name of Jesus through the centuries, it makes identifying with the name "Christian" difficult. When I am traveling, and a stranger asks, "What do you do?" I hesitate to tell them. Do I admit that I am a pastor? Do I openly claim the name of Jesus? Or do I simply say, "Well, I am in the people business." People have strong opinions concerning Christians in the United States of America and they wonder, What does it look like to authentically follow Jesus?

Perhaps that was the question Joseph and Nicodemus were asking themselves as they watched Jesus being put on trial. As he was being questioned by Caiaphas, did they seek out the truth? Did they attempt to bring reason into the conversation? Were others aware of their sympathy toward Jesus's cause? It is not hard for me to imagine that certain members of the Sanhedrin were not notified of this sinister gathering in the middle of the night, a strange time for religious tribunals to take place:

> *So the soldiers, their officer, and the Jewish police arrested Jesus*
> *and bound him. First they took him to Annas, who was the*
> *father-in-law of Caiaphas, the high priest that year. Caiaphas*
> *was the one who had advised the Jews that it was better to have*
> *one person die for the people.*
>
> John 18:12-14

What if neither Joseph nor Nicodemus was invited to the trial? If that was the case, when they heard of the trial, they realized their protests were too late. They could not persuade the decision of the ruling council. And once Pilate was involved, surely for Nicodemus and Joseph all hope was lost. They had witnessed what trifling with Rome did, along roadways on the outskirts of towns, bodies hanging, would-be rebels nailed to trees signaling "here's your end if you mess with Rome."

All of this is imaginative. We are left to fill in the gaps left by Scripture. It is hard to know: did Joseph and Nicodemus preserve their power through deafening silence or were they cut out of the discussion because of their passion for Jesus? They do not seem like model followers of Jesus. And yet I am compelled to recognize that Joseph and Nicodemus did show up. Even if John's Gospel might place a shroud of doubt over their personal faith, they were there.

Ministry of Presence

The ministry of presence is no small act. I have reminded numerous persons in conversation when they are walking through the valley that God promises to be with us, "Yea, though I walk through the valley of the shadow of death, I will fear no evil:

for thou art with me; thy rod and thy staff they comfort me" (Psalm 23:4 KJV). I cannot help quoting it in the King James Version of the Bible. It is a reminder that God is present even in our suffering. God promises to be with us, and as followers of Jesus we are called to walk with one another in our suffering and grief. And that is where we find Nicodemus and Joseph:

> *They took the body of Jesus and wrapped it with the spices in linen cloths, according to the burial custom of the Jews. Now there was a garden in the place where he was crucified, and in the garden there was a new tomb in which no one had ever been laid. And so, because it was the Jewish day of Preparation and the tomb was nearby, they laid Jesus there.*
>
> John 19:40-42

There really is something sacred about simply showing up. The ministry of presence is a holy, intentional act of being with one another, especially in life's darkest moments. When words fail, when answers do not come easy, when the valley of the shadow of death stretches long before us, our presence with one another becomes the most powerful gift we can offer one another. Followers of Jesus sit in hospital rooms. Disciples hold hands at gravesides. And we show up at the doorstep with a meal. We do not engage in the ministry of presence to fix the situation. We do not show up to explain the right next steps. No, Reader, we are simply there *to be* present. Because in these times, our greatest offering is not our wisdom, but our willingness to walk beside someone in their grief.

In his "My Parting Prescription for America," former United States Surgeon General, Dr. Vivek Murthy reminded readers of our deep need for community. Sometimes in a culture that celebrates lone rangers and single achievers, we need to embrace our independence as a human community. And the only way to build community is through love. Murthy wrote, "The love required to build community must not be reserved only for close family and friends or those who share our beliefs and life experiences; it must also be extended to neighbors, colleagues, people of different backgrounds, people with whom we disagree, and even people we consider our opponents. It requires recognizing something deeper and more fundamental that connects us."[1]

This love that Dr. Murthy talked about is not a sentimental, fleeting kind of love. This brand of love binds us together. Love is generous, kind, and courageous. It is the love that refuses to be transactional and that does not require close friendship or stop short of those who do not think like us, vote like us, or live like us. It is a love that extends across the street to the neighbor we do not understand. This love embraces the coworker who challenges us. It is a love that transforms our understanding of the person we once called our enemy. It is Jesus's demonstration of love; love that sits at the table with tax collectors, zealots, women, outsiders, and sinners. Jesus's love is a love that stretches arms out wide on a cross for those who mocked and betrayed him. Jesus's love is a radical invitation into community, where the curious convert and the courageous and adversaries become allies.

Perhaps Joseph and Nicodemus did not embrace Jesus's form of communal love at first. Maybe they were silent in the face of opposition. But in the aftermath of Jesus's arrest, trial, and crucifixion they showed up. These men took a risk. It was risky to ask for the body of their friend, having no idea how Pilate would respond:

After these things, Joseph of Arimathea, who was a disciple of Jesus, though a secret one because of his fear of the Jews, asked Pilate to let him take away the body of Jesus. Pilate gave him permission, so he came and removed his body. Nicodemus, who had at first come to Jesus by night, also came, bringing a mixture of myrrh and aloes, weighing about a hundred pounds. They took the body of Jesus and wrapped it with the spices in linen cloths, according to the burial custom of the Jews.

John 19:38-40

One hundred pounds of spices is an excessive amount for the preparation of Jesus's body. Remember how Mary of Bethany in John 12 was chastised by Judas for using one pound of pure nard? If this disturbed the disciples, just imagine one hundred pounds! Although some people interpret this extravagance as a sign that Joseph and Nicodemus affirmed Jesus's death, others suggest that this amount was used in preparation for a king. In his article, "From Darkness to Light: Nicodemus, 'the Jews' and John's Gospel," Alexander James Reedrow suggested, "Instead, it is more likely that Nicodemus's spices are meant to portray him in a positive light, and a number of intertexts both within and without the gospel are suggestive to this end. Outside of the gospel, the vast quantity of spices is easily paralleled with the lavishness of royal burials attested in other ancient literature. The theme of kingship is one native to John's depiction of Jesus, especially in the passion narrative, so that we may interpret Nicodemus's actions, and that of his companion, and say, 'They have, in effect, affirmed Pilate's inscription 'Jesus of Nazareth [is] king of the Jews.'"[2] Could it be that in the courageous asking, the careful transporting, the costly preparing, and the eventual laying to rest that Nicodemus and Joseph were making a declaration? Jesus of Nazareth was now their king. In this caring act they were protesting the actions of the Romans. Could this investment of tomb and time be the signal of their fullhearted commitment to Jesus as Lord?

Joseph and Nicodemus were unlikely allies and their place in the Crucifixion story brings us to a significant question: Could this be you? Could it be that you or I have spent time living as a secret disciple? Perhaps we have lacked vocabulary or voice, allowing obligations or distractions to keep us from truly following? Instead of beating yourself up, maybe today is the day you courageously find your voice and invest in Jesus's mission. Maybe today's the day you give yourself fullheartedly to the one who did the same for you.

Unlikely You

What I love about Joseph and Nicodemus is that they eventually show up, speak up, and stand up for Jesus. Their motives do not always seem clear. They did not even confess their sins that we are aware of; and there is no "I believe" spoken from their lips. In Joseph of Arimathea and Nicodemus there was just action. For all the responsible ones, the doing ones, the ones who feel comfortable with tools in their hands and sweat dripping from their brows, these two men gift you with a spiritual path to follow. These doers stand up for the good of all that is human, and the ministry of presence.

God calls the most unlikely people to stand in the gap for those who cannot speak for themselves, for those who require another human to stand up for justice, peace, or reconciliation. God calls them to pick up the mic, to intentionally form community, and to mobilize the protest. Of course, God calls people like Daryl Davis to be unlikely allies, but God calls so many others as well. Over the last several years I have encountered people stepping out of their usual spheres of influence and partnering with the unlikely to form an alliance. Rev. Dr. Heber Brown began to imagine what he could do with the fifteen hundred square feet of grass behind his church. He did not have a green thumb, and yet with the partnership of a more seasoned woman in his congregation, they began to plant seeds of hope behind the church. In the aftermath of racial unrest in Baltimore, that community garden began to feed the city. And they never imagined it would foster a network of over 250 Black churches and 150 Black farmers. Brown launched the Black Church Food Security Network, defying a broken food system with soil-stained hands and Spirit-filled hearts throughout the United States.

Dr. Aaron Kuecker was not expected to make waves. As president of the small and often-overlooked Trinity Christian College, he could have stayed the course. But instead, he and his team cut college tuition by 40 percent! They did not want students to graduate with an albatross of debt, so they were determined to create solutions to a system-wide problem. Trinity then partnered with local organizations to connect students to real careers, solving real-world problems, living out the gospel not in theory but in practice.

Joshua Hayashi was not your typical church developer. Ordained in 2014 in the Disciples of Christ and living in Hawaii, he saw the writing on the wall. One hundred thousand churches will close by 2050 throughout the United States of America. Instead of wallowing in despair, he imagined partnering with people to dream of something new. He brought kingdom-minded developers together to reimagine sacred spaces, not as private property, but as public goods. Determined to keep land for the people, he wanted to ensure churches reimagined one of their best assets.

Cristin Cooper was not aiming to start a movement. She just wanted folks to experience more than a Sunday service. She started with soup and gathering people around her kitchen table. Her dinner church, now known as Coop's Soups, has become a spiritual table where local growers, markets, and food pantries collaborate to nourish both body and soul. Its mission is simple: to make soup worth sharing. It is truly "belonging in a bowl."

Chelsea Spyres, when working for Riverfront Ministries, saw a commercial kitchen that sat empty all week. Where most church leaders saw a gap, she experienced an opportunity. She built a cooperative between local businesses and a congregation, transforming a quiet church commercial kitchen into a buzzing hub for economic empowerment and shared mission in Wilmington Kitchen Collective.

Beverly Jenkins had a vision not for charity, but for dignity. On a mission trip to Haiti, where she believed that she was bringing Jesus, was prompted by the Spirit to stop asking, "What do these people need?" and began asking, "What do they *want?*" What followed was nothing short of miraculous: R&R Marketplace. R&R Marketplace in Dellwood, Missouri, is a space so Spirit-led that even the bank that once denied her a loan now rents space inside it.

Joe Bowling had no fancy degrees, merely a deep calling to the neighborhood. He moved back to Englewood, Indiana, where his father pastored a church that had historic ties to the KKK. He rooted himself in the same soil that had borne generations of pain, repented of the harm that had been done, and through unlikely partnerships, including Purdue University, helped launch a magnet school where the robotics team is now ranked eleventh in the world. That is just like God. God uses the overlooked, teams up the unexpected, and through holy collaboration, fosters a future that no one person could have dreamed alone.

What about you? What about us? The world is still in desperate need of unlikely humans. We need people who will stand where others step aside, speak when silence is easy, and love when hate feels inevitable. God has always used ordinary people to do extraordinary work. As you think about unlikely partnership, just imagine your neighborhood. Is there an injustice that makes your heart burn? Could you be the person who starts a hard conversation where reconciliation is needed in your family, your church, or your community? You do not have to be famous. You do not have to be powerful. You merely have to say yes to following Jesus. God uses unlikely you to partner people together to do work on this side of heaven. The result? Maybe, just maybe, together we will experience resurrection.

Practice: Take a Stand

In your small group or while engaged in worship, instruct persons to write commitments on Post-it notes or small pieces of paper. Invite people to prayerfully consider the ways in which God is asking them to step up as unlikely allies. Prompt the writer with a scenario where God is calling them to show up and practice the ministry of presence. Maybe there is an injustice they notice in their neighborhood, city, region, or around the world that they feel stirred to stand up for. Perhaps God is prompting them to become a kingdom solution to a kingdom problem in the church they serve. Or maybe they simply want to grow in their faith and move from cautious curiosity to courageous commitment.

Create a sacred space where people can bring forward these commitments and simply place them or nail them to a cross. Ask them to write them down. Their commitment could be a word, phrase, or sentence. Give ample time for people to reflect on their commitments. Encourage those who are processors to take their pieces of paper home and prayerfully consider what the Spirit may be asking them to do. Much like Joseph of Arimathea and Nicodemus, their penning these words becomes an act of surrender, courage, and a public declaration that "Jesus is my King and my Lord." Also encourage people with the knowledge that God will never send them alone. They are partnered together for God's kingdom purposes. God will form unlikely allies in the most unlikely of spaces.

God of the unlikely, much like Joseph and Nicodemus, we can find ourselves having a cautious faith, and yet you call us to move from caution to courage. Keep moving in our hearts and in our calendars so that we can love our neighbors in tangible ways. Make clear the means by which we are called to reconcile, to stand, and to commit to your work of justice in the world. Amen.

EPILOGUE

I love a good spring cleaning. Recently my husband, Jon, and I decided to tackle the garage. With limited space we determined it was time to rummage through the boxes we had been holding on to for the last twenty years. That's right, twenty years including, but not limited to, four moves, three extra kiddos, a high school graduation, and more packing tape than we could possibly imagine. As we began to open the boxes, we realized there were stacks of T-shirts from college that held a faint recollection, a promise that I would turn them into some kind of blanket keepsake. By now these T-shirts had yellowed, and the plastic lettering was so brittle it was cracking. The box containing remnants of our wedding was another small museum: wedding cards from people Jon and I cannot quite remember, programs from the ceremony, and we had even kept our cake topper complete with icing crusted on the bottom. I was shocked that it was not crawling with ants. "What were we thinking? Why did we keep this stuff?" I questioned Jon. There were so many boxes full of things that we should have thrown away years ago. This probably does not happen at your house. But sometimes we just cling to stuff that no longer serves us. And that is just what has been hanging out in our storage spaces.

What about when life gets messy, and tomorrow is unsure, what do you cling to then? Sometimes it is hard to move forward into unknown spaces. Sometimes it is hard to picture that tomorrow's best-case scenario could outdo today's worse-case situation of old comforts stored in time-worn boxes. Sometimes we just want to hold on to what we know!

Early in the morning Mary had come to the tomb to finish the burial preparations on Jesus's body. Head down, hostage to the many thoughts racing through her mind, she did not see the open tomb at first, but when she did, she ran to tell Peter and Jesus's beloved disciple. After an abrupt foot race between the two men, Mary reappeared on the scene, setting out to do all the things she knew to do.

Stuck in the Tomb

Mary of Magdala had come with a plan. She came expecting to use the spices and oils that she had brought. Mary was determined to find Jesus's body and prepare it for the long slumber of death. She knew what to do, a tangible offering of love for the deceased.

Did Mary wonder what this would mean for her, for her past, and for her future? Staring at an empty tomb, Mary was not merely mourning Jesus, she was mourning the life she had just begun to experience. Mary was grieving the future she believed in. This was a woman who had been radically transformed by Jesus. According to Luke, Jesus had cast seven demons out of her and whether that meant demons of illness, oppression, or something deeper we are not quite sure. What we do know is that she had been bound by something dark, and Jesus had truly set her free:

Soon afterward he went on through one town and village after another, proclaiming and bringing the good news of the kingdom of God. The twelve were with him, as well as some women who had been cured of evil spirits and infirmities: Mary, called Magdalene, from whom seven demons had gone out, and Joanna, the wife of Herod's steward Chuza, and Susanna, and many others, who ministered to them out of their own resources.

Luke 8:1-3

It was no wonder she followed him with such devotion. Jesus had given her a new life, a new purpose, and a new destiny. That was until now. With his death her life felt ripped away. It makes sense that she would be clinging to the past. She had built her world around Jesus, and now she felt paralyzed in the grief of remembering the way things used to be. Perhaps you can relate. Have you ever found yourself caught up in the tomb of nostalgia, longing for the way things used to be? You long for the simple delights of your childhood. You pine over life when your parents were alive, when you loved your partner, or when your kids were little. You long for the day when people were kinder, politics less divisive, and the world not merely as troubling. Some of us are holding so tight to what we know that we are afraid to step into what is next. We keep attempting to make sure everything stays the same, because if we navigate one more change, we may just lose our minds.

Mary could not see what was right in front of her. Was she blinded by grief? Was it shame? Was it regret?

But Mary stood weeping outside the tomb. As she wept, she bent over to look into the tomb, and she saw two angels in white sitting where the body of Jesus had been lying, one at the head and the other at the feet. They said to her, "Woman, why are you weeping?" She said to them, "They have taken away my Lord, and I do not know where they have laid him."

John 20:11-13

Mary's tears were not just a few silent tears. Mary was full-on ugly crying. You know what I am describing. The kind of grief where your vision blurs, your chest heaves, and snot runs down your face. The kind of sorrow that makes everything hazy, where you could not even see straight, let alone recognize that the figures sitting inside the tomb were angels. Maybe she wiped at her face, trying to make sense of what she was witnessing, but the weight of sorrow was too much. Her heart was shattered, her hope was buried and now, to make matters worse, even Jesus's body was gone. She was drowning so deeply in loss that when the angels asked why she was crying, she could barely muster an answer. They were messengers of heaven, glowing in divine presence, but to Mary, they were just figures in the blur of her grief.

But Reader, the story does not end there. When Mary turned around there was a man standing close by and she assumed he was the gardener. But he was not. It was Jesus, and he was alive. Jesus immediately spoke her name, "Mary!" And Mary grabbed for him. *Oh, my goodness, Jesus! Don't ever leave me again! I've been so scared! You have no idea!* But what Jesus said next was some of the most interesting and unexpected words. "Do not hold on to me, for I have not yet ascended to the Father. Go instead to my brothers and tell them, 'I am ascending to my Father and your Father, to my God and your God'" (John 20:17 NIV).

Don't Cling

What a strange response coming from Jesus! Don't hold on to me, don't cling to me, really? This was just not like Jesus. Jesus was the guy who welcomed children and who ate dinner elbow to elbow next to everyone. If you keep on reading through the Gospel of John, you'll see that Jesus invited Thomas, the disciple with trust issues, to not merely touch his resurrected body but to put his fingers in the holes left from the nails. What was this about Jesus? Of course, Mary was going to grab Jesus as soon as she recognized him. Can you blame her?

She had assumed Jesus was gone forever. She believed life as she knew it was over. Everything she had built her hope around had been buried in that tomb. And now against all odds Jesus was back. Can you imagine the emotional whiplash? The grief, the despair, the heartbreak and then all of those emotions were instantly replaced by shock, wonder, and joy. So she did what any of us would do when we think we have finally gotten back what we lost. Mary tried to hold on! Desperate, relieved, and overwhelmed, she grabbed for Jesus like she was never letting go. But Jesus said, "Don't!"

Not because Jesus did not love Mary, nor because he did not understand how she felt, but because another plan was unfolding. Mary was holding on to what was, when God was calling her into what was next. Mary wanted to freeze that moment, to go back to the Jesus she knew, but resurrection is not about going back. Resurrection is about moving forward. Jesus is alive, but he is not alive so we can all stay the same. He was calling Mary to step into the wild, unfolding future of God's kingdom. And maybe that is the word some of us need: stop clinging to what was and start stepping into what God is doing next. Stop clinging to what was never meant to be permanent.

What might you be holding on to? Are you clinging to a relationship that is over, but you keep holding on? Do you have a life direction that has changed but you keep trying to force it, holding on to the old? You have always been a parent, but now your kids crave independence, and you are just not ready to let go. Perhaps you have a version of faith that felt solid for decades, but now there's a holy discontent rising in you. God is inviting you into something deeper but you long for what was, unable to picture what could be. Jesus was not calling Mary to go back to what she had experienced before. Jesus was calling her forward into something new. Mary's best prayer was for restoration, and she could not yet envision resurrection.

Embrace an Unlikely Faith

Mary had what I am calling an unlikely faith. She was not the one people would have picked to be the first preacher of the Resurrection. She had lived a complicated past and was now experiencing a whole lot of confusion about what was happening with Jesus. If there was a vote on who should get the honor of announcing the greatest news in history, Mary's name would not have even been on the ballot. And yet God chose her. Jesus did not wait for the most popular, the most experienced, or the most put-together person to be his witness. Jesus empowered the one who had been broken, the one who had doubted, and the one who was not even supposed to be there. And if that's how faith works, then maybe Jesus is calling you too.

And here's the thing about this unlikely faith: it shows up in the places we least expect. You see, Mary was not the only one. Throughout history, Jesus has continued to reveal himself to the overlooked ones, the struggling ones, the ones who suffer, and the ones who feel like their story disqualifies them from ever being loved by God. Reader, could that be you?

I invite you to simply trust that Jesus is alive. Trust that Jesus sees you, and that Jesus is calling you forward. Jesus is standing right in front of you, calling your name. Maybe today is the day you stop clinging to what was and start stepping into what's next. Perhaps it's time to let go of those old boxes, to throw away those worn-out T-shirts, and to make room for new possibilities in your life. If you have been holding on to the past, today is the day to let go. Jesus is meeting you where you are, right here, right now. Are you ready to embrace an unlikely faith?

Jesus, help me to let go. When I am tempted to clench my fist around everything that I know, help me to open my hands, my heart, and my calendar to new life possibilities. When fear tells me to cling to what's familiar, give me courage to trust you with the unknown. Remind me that you are present, preparing space for me to grow, to love, and to live more fully. Help me believe that resurrection is possible and that even now, you are calling my name and inviting me into an unlikely faith. Amen.

NOTES

Chapter 1

1 Pete Enns, host, *The Bible for Normal People*, podcast, episode 245, "Elizabeth Schrader Polczer—Resurrecting Mary the Tower," May 15, 2023, https://thebiblefornormalpeople.com/episode-245-elizabeth -schrader-polczer-resurrecting-mary-the-tower/.

Chapter 2

1 Daniel Herman, "The Tyrian Shekel: The Temple Tax Coin in the Time of Jesus," https://dannythedigger.com/the-temple-tax-coin-in-the-time -of-jesus/.

2 F. Scott Spencer, "Out of Mind, Out of Voice: Slave-Girls and Prophetic Daughters in Luke-Acts," *Biblical Interpretation* 7, no. 2 (1999): 138.

3 N. T. Wright and Michael F. Bird, *The New Testament in Its World* (Grand Rapids, MI: Zondervan Academic, 1999), 148–49.

4 Brown, Raymond E., Joseph A. Fitzmeyer, and Roland E. Murphy, eds., *The New Jerome Biblical Commentary* (Englewood Cliffs, NJ: Prentice Hall, 1990), 671.

Chapter 3

1 Wright and Bird, *The New Testament in Its World*, 92.

2 Wright and Bird, *The New Testament in Its World*, 128–31.

3 Wright and Bird, *The New Testament in Its World*, 131–36.

4 Wright and Bird, *The New Testament in Its World*, 132.

5 Wright and Bird, *The New Testament in Its World*, 122.

6 Robert L. Merritt, "Jesus Barabbas and the Paschal Pardon," *Journal of Biblical Literature* 104, no. 1 (1985): 58–60.

7   Tim Mackie and Jon Collins, "What Is the Day of Atonement?" *BibleProject*, produced by Cooper Peltz, July 4, 2022, transcript, https://bibleproject.com/podcasts/what-day-atonement/.

8   Brené Brown, *Daring Greatly: How the Courage to Be Vulnerable Transforms the Way We Live, Love, Parent, and Lead* (New York: Avery, 2015), 68.

Chapter 4

1   Shane Claiborne, Jonathan Wilson-Hartgrove, and Enuma Okoro, eds., *Common Prayer: A Liturgy for Ordinary Radicals* (Grand Rapids, MI: Zondervan, 2010), 74.

Chapter 5

1   Mary Rose D'Angelo, "Unnamed Women at The Cross," in *Women in Scripture: A Dictionary of Named and Unnamed Women in the Hebrew Bible, the Apocryphal/Deuterocanonical Books, and the New Testament*, ed. Carol Meyers (New York: Houghton Mifflin Harcourt, 2000), 421.

2   United Women in Faith, https://uwfaith.org/who-we-are/our-history/.

3   "Chiefs Kicker Butker Congratulates Women Graduates and Says Most Are More Excited About Motherhood," May 16, 2024, https://apnews.com/article/kansas-city-chiefs-harrison-butker-e00f6ee45955c99ef1e809ec447239e0.

4   Tom Wright, *John for Everyone, Part 2: Chapters 11–21* (London: SPCK, 2002), 129.

5   "The Baptismal Covenant I," *The United Methodist Hymnal* (Nashville: United Methodist Publishing House, 1989), 35.

6   James Wm. McClendon Jr, *Biography as Theology* (Nashville:Abingdon Press, 1974), 127–128.

Chapter 6

1   Vivek Murthy, "My Parting Prescription for America," January 7, 2025, 18, https://www.vivekmurthy.com/partingprescription.

2   Alexander James Reedrow, "From Darkness to Light: Nicodemus, 'the Jews' and John's Gospel," *Journal of Theological Interpretation* 18, no. 1 (2024): 89.

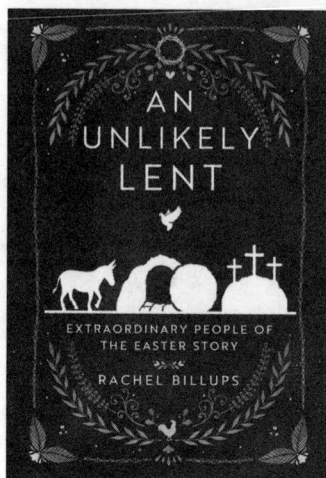